PARALEGAL CERTIFICATE COURSE

Legal Document Preparation Manual

THE CENTER FOR
LEGAL STUDIES

www.legalstudies.com

Paralegal Certificate Course© Legal Document Preparation Manual
By The Center for Legal Studies
©2013, The Center for Legal Studies
Printed in the United States of America.
The Center for Legal Studies

PREFACE

This book is designed to be used in conjunction with the Paralegal Certificate Course© and other paralegal studies courses to quickly and efficiently prepare paralegals. The notes and samples are designed to reinforce course lesson materials, and to help the student learn to apply the concepts and practical skills necessary for a successful paralegal career. Please note that any examples provided are for instructional purposes only and may not reflect proper formatting guidelines for all jurisdictions. As always, check your local rules of court for exact document specifications and filing requirements.

For information regarding Paralegal, Advanced Paralegal, Legal Investigation, Legal Nurse Consultant, Legal Secretary, Alternative Dispute Resolution, Victim Advocacy, Intellectual Property Law for Engineers, Personal Injury for Paralegals, Software Essentials for the Law Office, Advanced Legal Research and Writing Certificate Courses, or Standardized Test Preparation, please call The Center for Legal Studies at 303-273-9777 or toll-free at 1-800-522-7737. Visit us online at www.legalstudies.com.

TABLE OF CONTENTS

Chapter One: Introduction to Legal Document Preparation

Document preparation, using either a word processing program or specialized document generation software, remains one of the common tasks undertaken by paralegals. It is paramount that the document preparer possesses a fundamental understanding of the rules of law that apply to a particular document and its sections.

There exists a wide array of legal documents that differ in both nature and function. Some documents (such as pleadings, motions, orders and appellate briefs) are filed with the court. Others (such as discovery requests, contracts, or real estate documents) are not generally filed with the court but are still subject to common-practice or rule-imposed format and content specifications. Specific format and layout requirements may vary widely from office to office and court to court, but the basic elements of most documents remain consistent throughout the legal world.

GENERAL DOCUMENT FORMATTING GUIDELINES

Barring court rules or specific office preferences, the following formatting guidelines can be followed:

Paper size

Historically all legal documents were prepared on legal size paper (8.5 by 14 inches). In an effort to be uniform, most courts now require 8.5 by 11 inch white bond paper for all pleadings. Documents should be one sided. Be sure to check the local court rules for the appropriate jurisdiction to make sure that your documents are in compliance.

Font size and face

Generally, a 12 point font is preferred. Common font faces are Courier, Times New Roman, or Arial.

Margins

The top margin should be 2 inches for the first page and 1.5 inches for subsequent pages. The left margin on all pages should be 1.5 inches for all left aligned text. The first line of a new paragraph should be indented 1 inch or ten spaces from the left margin. In general, the right margin should be between .75 inches and 1 inch with the exception of the end of a paragraph. See Figure 1. Using your word processing program, you can justify the text to allow for the right margin to be uniformly aligned. Justification is optional but if you choose to justify make sure the right margin is 1 inch. The bottom margin for legal documents should be at least 1 inch from the bottom of the page. Be sure to leave room for pagination and/or signatures.

Spacing

Text should be double-spaced. However, there are some exceptions. Do not double space addresses, property descriptions or quotes indented within the body of a document. These should be single spaced instead. *See Figure 4.* Triple spacing should be used after headings and between party identifications.

Page Numbering

Do not number the first page of the document but do number all subsequent pages. The page number usually appears in the middle of the page, or in the lower right corner.

Paragraph Placement

Paragraphs continuing on the following page should include at least two lines of text on each page. Three line paragraphs should not be divided, but instead, should simply begin on the subsequent page. If carrying the text over to the next page leaves a gap of white space, simply enter [END OF TEXT ON THIS PAGE].

Signatures

All court documents must be signed, frequently by more than one individual and signature lines must be provided. The name of the person (and capacity or title where applicable) whose signature will appear should be accurately typed below the signature line. All signatures should appear on the same page, and all signature pages must include at least two lines of text to avoid any opportunity for, or appearance of, impropriety. Agreements are signed by all parties. If a party is signing on behalf of a company or other entity, the entity's name needs to be placed 3 spaces above the signature line. The individual's capacity should also be reflected. *See Figure 1.*

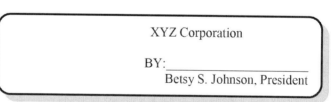

FIGURE 1: Party Signature line

Other documents may require the need for witness signatures and/or court personnel, so be sure to research your local court rules for your jurisdictions requirements. Attorneys may sign some documents on behalf of the party.

Most court documents include some common elements: the caption, the body or text, the signature block or subscription and the certificate of service or mailing.

The caption is the formal heading of a legal document appearing at the top of the page, and includes the name of the court in which the Complaint will be filed, the names and designation of the parties involved in the matter and the case number.   The court heading is generally aligned with the left margin or centered on the document depending on court rules. The case number is provided to the right of the party names.   The court name, the party names and the words identifying the case number (also commonly referred to as the Index Number, or Docket Number) are generally keyed in all caps.

STATE OF NEW YORK
SUPREME COURT: COUNTY OF ERIE

JANE DOE,   **COMPLAINT**

            Plaintiff,

                                                         INDEX NO: _____

v.
 ROBERT ROE,
                  Defendant.

FIGURE 2: Example Caption

Some jurisdictions require the court heading to appear between 5-8 lines below the attorney's name, state bar number also known as the attorney registration number, address, and telephone number.

Attorney Name, Registration Number
Attorney Address
City, State, ZIP
Phone Number (with area code)

                                    SUPERIOR COURT OF THE STATE OF CALIFORNIA
                                      FOR THE COUNTY OF SACRAMENTO

NAME OF PLAINTIFF,   CASE NO.: 12-3-456789-1

            Plaintiff,   REQUEST FOR
                                          ADMISSIONS

    v.

NAME OF DEFENDANT,

            Defendant

FIGURE 3: Example Caption 2

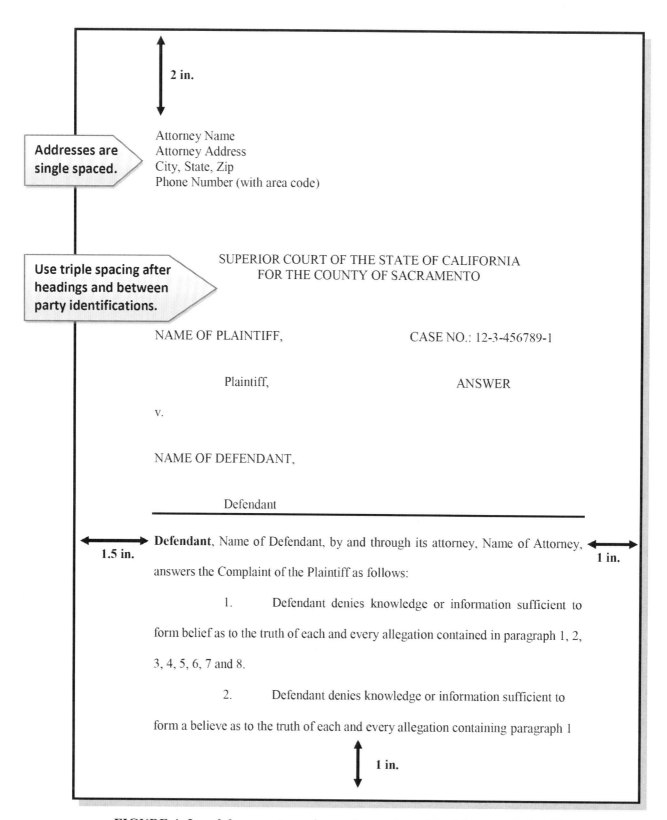

FIGURE 4: Legal document spacing and margins with right margin justified

With the increase in electronic filing, several jurisdictions now have preformatted captions available on their websites. There are options to download captions, copy and paste captions into a document, or simply type in the information in the caption just like filling out an online form. *See Figure 5.* Make sure to set your margins according to the court rules before copying the caption to your document.

Note: Be sure to save your caption, as it will be required on nearly all subsequent documents prepared in the case! While most captions paralegals have to fill in will be simply "plaintiff" and "defendant", pay close attention to titles when litigation drags on. The case name may actually change with the addition, subtraction, or death of parties and a case with multiple pleadings and cross-motions can quickly confuse a paralegal.

Attorney or Party without attorney (name, state bar # and address) Phone: Fax: Email: Attorney for (name):	
Court Court Address	▼ For Court Use Only ▼
Insert appropriate party names and designations	Case Number: _____
TITLE OF FORM	

FIGURE 5: Example Pre-formatted Caption

Many jurisdictions now also have pleading forms that you may be required to use. Whenever you need to file anything with a court, always check to see if there is a form for your exact legal problem. Some forms are adopted (meaning their use is mandatory) and some are approved (using them is optional). If using an optional form you must still provide the information requested on the form, but you can use a different form or write the information without using a form. Forms are either federal forms, state forms or local forms. Most forms used in court are state forms and are on the state judicial branch's court website. Federal forms, if adopted, will be on the corresponding federal court website. Local forms are usually available on your local court's website. If necessary, call or go to the clerk's office and ask for the local form you need. Always verify that you have the most current edition of the form.

The body or text of most court documents states facts, sets forth specific allegations, or makes requests through separate numbered paragraphs, to which the opposing party may easily and directly respond.   The body generally begins with a preamble identifying the plaintiff and the purpose of the document.   Note that the initial word or phrase is frequently provided in all caps.

> THE PLAINTIFF, by and through his attorney, Arthur Johnston, states the following Complaint against the Defendants:

FIGURE 6: Example Introductory Preamble for Complaint

> **COMES NOW,** the plaintiff, John Doe by and through his Attorney Arthur Johnston, and pursuant to Ohio State Rules of Civil Procedure, requests Defendant, Robert Roe admit or deny the following.

FIGURE 7: Example Introductory Preamble for Discovery

The body then goes on to either specify allegations, or make specific requests of the recipient through a series of chronologically numbered paragraphs.   Text constituting the body of the document is generally double-spaced, with the first line of each paragraph indented five or ten spaces from the left margin.

> 1.   On July 7, 2008 at approximately 3:30 a.m., Plaintiff Jane Doe was the driver of a 2007 Honda Civic traveling northbound on Peachtree Avenue in Pleasantville, Florida.
>
> 2.   On the same date and time, Defendant Robert Roe was the driver of a 1976 Ford Mustang traveling westbound on Smithport Road in Pleasantville, Florida.
>
> 3.   Plaintiffs' vehicle was at a stop on Peachtree Avenue at its intersection with Smithport Road. While Plaintiffs' vehicle was at a stop, the vehicle being driven by Defendant Roe struck the rear of the Plaintiff's vehicle.
>
> 4.   The impact of the collision pushed Plaintiffs' vehicle forward causing it to strike the vehicle in front of it.

FIGURE 8: Example Body of Complaint

CHAPTER ONE | 13

1. Admit that you were personally served with the Writ of Summons and Complaint in the above-captioned case.

2. Admit that a resident of your household was personally served with the Writ of Summons and Complaint.

3. Admit that you have no basis to assert as a defense or affirmative defense to the subject accident, lack of personal jurisdiction.

FIGURE 9: Example Body of Request for Admissions

The attorney's signature block should include the name, address and telephone number of the attorney providing representation. Some jurisdictions also require the attorney's state bar identification number. The law firm and identification of the party represented is generally provided 3 – 4 spaces above the signature line, but this may vary based on attorney preference. In signing the document, the attorney certifies that the facts alleged in the Complaint are true to the best of his or her knowledge and that existing law supports the allegations.

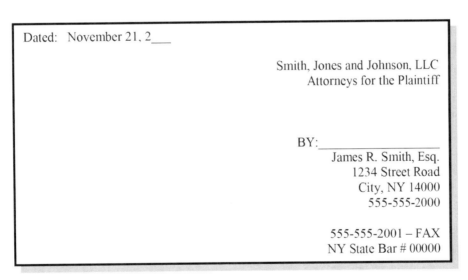

Dated: November 21, 2___

Smith, Jones and Johnson, LLC
Attorneys for the Plaintiff

BY:_____
James R. Smith, Esq.
1234 Street Road
City, NY 14000
555-555-2000

555-555-2001 – FAX
NY State Bar # 00000

FIGURE 10: Example Attorney Signature Block

The Certificate of Service (or Mailing) denotes proof that you actually mailed (served) a copy of your document to an agency or person (interested party) or their legal counsel. This should be included with each document subsequent to the Complaint.

CERTIFICATE OF SERVICE

I, James R. Smith, attorney for Plaintiff do hereby certify that a true and correct copy of the Plaintiff's Request for Documents Production was served, upon Counsel to Defendant by first class mail via U.S. Postal Service to the last known address known to me this ____day of _____, 2____ addressed as follows:

Regina Randolph, Registration # 667
6868 Pothole Rd.
Amherst, NY 00101
(555) 555-5551

FIGURE 11: Example Certificate of Service

These are just some of the common elements in pleadings and legal documents. We will cover pleadings extensively in Chapter 3 and discovery in Chapter 4.

Chapter Two: Contracts

Christina Miranda, Esq.

Contract law is one area of law most people are familiar with, though they may not realize it. Contracts are prevalent in daily life: rental agreements, mortgages for a home, employment contracts, cell phone contracts, the agreement with a neighbor's kid to mow your lawn, etc. As a paralegal, you may be asked to review, summarize, or even draft contracts. Insight into this subject will not only help you to sharpen your legal skills but sharpen your life skills as well.

INTRODUCTION TO CONTRACTS

At its most basic level, a <u>contract</u> is an agreement between two parties to do something or not do something. If promises are made and not met, the contract is broken and the law will provide a remedy. A contract represents a <u>bargained-for exchange</u> supported by <u>consideration</u>.

Terminology

Before beginning our discussion of contracts it is helpful to review some vocabulary terms. An <u>offeror</u> is the party who begins the contract negotiating process. The offeror may make his offer in the form of a question such as "will you take $1,500.00 for your beat up old Nissan Sentra?" The offeror may submit a proposal as an independent contractor stating, "I will complete your bathroom tile work for $700.00 plus expenses".

> You might be thinking of consumer purchases you make every day like buying groceries, clothes, or furniture. But purchases of consumer goods or even industrial goods like tractors and widgets have their own area of law known as <u>sales</u>. The law of sales is governed by the Uniform Commercial Code (UCC). This is separate from our discussion of contract law.

The person to whom the offer is being made is the offeree. The <u>offeree</u> is given the choice of accepting the offer or not accepting the offer. In the example above, the owner of the Nissan Sentra is the offeree of the $1,500.00 payment that is suggested by the offeror.

Performance is a contract term that trips up many students. In contract law, performance does refer to the artistic manner of singing, dancing, or acting in a play. According to Black's Law Dictionary, "<u>Performance</u> is the fulfillment or accomplishment of a promise, contract, or other obligation according to the agreed upon terms". The payment of $1,500.00 for the Nissan and the subsequent delivery of the title and keys to the car constitute performance of the agreement above. Similarly, completed tile work in the bathroom is the performance of the contract proposed in our second example.

Other terms you will want to familiarize yourself with include unilateral and bilateral. While modern contract law refrains from using the terms unilateral and bilateral, you will work with attorneys of all ages and legal backgrounds that still frequently use these terms. You will also encounter case law and statutes that still distinguish contracts on this basis.

A unilateral contract is a one-sided contract, which at its most basic level seeks a completed performance. The offeree can decide not to accept and is, in fact, not obligated to do anything at all. An example of a unilateral contract would be an offer for a $100 reward to find you neighbor's lost dog. You are not compelled to find the lost dog and the neighbor can't force you to do so. However, finding the lost dog would constitute acceptance and the neighbor would be liable to pay the reward.

Most contracts are bilateral contracts (i.e. business contracts, rental agreements, or prenuptial agreements). In a bilateral contract, the offeror and offeree exchange promises. If you offer to pay your neighbor's kid $10 for raking the leaves out of your yard, that would be a unilateral contract. You only pay the kid if the yard is raked and the kid has not promised to do anything. A bilateral contract would be if you promise to walk the neighbor kid's dog while she is at camp in exchange for her raking the leaves out of your yard. Both parties are making promises to do or not do something.

Contracts can be verbal or written. In the example above, it would be time consuming and unnecessary to write out a contract for dog walking and leaf raking. However, there are some contracts which **must** be written in order to be valid. This is known as the doctrine of the Statute of Frauds. According to this doctrine, contracts for the following matters should be in writing: transfer or sale of real estate or land (no matter the value), contracts for marriage, wills, contracts for personal services, contracts worth more than $500, and contracts which will take more than one year to complete. Given that a good deal of contracts are required to be in writing, it is essential that the paralegal understand the elements of a valid contract and is familiar with the common sections of a contract.

Elements of a Contract

In any contract, it is imperative that the intentions of the parties and any agreement reached between the parties be clearly expressed in easily understood language. You do not want any ambiguity. While the subject matter of a contract is virtually unlimited, all contracts must contain required elements to be valid. The easiest way to remember the essential

NOTE: Both parties must also have the capacity to enter into a contract for a contract to be legally enforceable.

parts of a contract is the acronym TACO: terms, acceptance, consideration, and offer. If any one of these components is missing you do not have a contract. Rather, you have a failed agreement which is not enforceable in a court of law.

The Offer

Every contract agreement begins with an offer. An <u>offer</u> is a statement which communicates to the offeree a willingness to enter an agreement; it is a <u>manifestation of intent</u> to enter into a contract and to be bound by the terms of the contract. Note that an offer is rarely titled something obvious like "offer". In order to be valid, the offer must be definite and must contain at least some essential and material terms:

1. specific quantity or date of completion
2. certain price or amount to be paid
3. parties intend to be bound by the contract
4. definite description of the subject of the contract

An offer must be communicated to a party who is identifiable. That means it must be clear who the offer is being made to whether in writing, telephone conversation, face to face meeting, or even email address and greeting. An offer cannot be a joke, boast, expression of anger, or exaggeration because a reasonable person would not expect that the person making such statements intends to bind themselves to the promises made in those statements. Is the person who is supposedly making the offer intending to be bound to sell something, make a promise, or to perform some act in return for an acceptance? An offer invites acceptance and, in fact, acceptance of the offer will conclude a bargain and form an agreement. Advertisements are considered to be invitations to offers because they are widely disseminated and contain very little definitive description. They are not usually addressed to anyone in particular. Unless there is an indication of exactly how many items are available for a particular price, ads invite consumers to walk into a store, find an item, and offer a price to complete a purchase.

Acceptance

The <u>acceptance</u> of an offer is the approval or agreement of the offeree to the offer, together with any and all of the offers' terms. In order for an acceptance to be valid certain rules must be upheld.

> ***Mirror image*** - Changing the price or details of the offer terminates the original offer and creates a new one (known as a counteroffer), which may or may not be accepted. The common law rule of contracts states that an offer must have an acceptance which is a mirror image, with the same terms and conditions as the offer, in order to be valid.

Aware - Before performing the contract the offeree must actually be aware of the offer. For example, Megan was going to offer her roommate Laurie $50 to wash the dishes when Laurie got home from work. She wrote a note to Laurie making this offer. The dog, Ginger, thinks notebook paper is tasty and ate the note. When Laurie arrived home, Megan was in the shower and Laurie decided to wash the dishes. Laurie is not owed $50 for washing the dishes because Laurie was not aware of Megan's offer.

Person - The person (or group) to whom the original offer was made to is the only person (or group) who can accept the offer. Using the previous example, the third roommate, Ellen arrives home just in time to grab the note from Ginger's mouth. Ellen reads the note, thinks, "good deal!" and washes the dishes. Megan does not owe Ellen $50 for washing the dishes because only Laurie could have accepted the offer.

Notice of performance – Notice of performance of a unilateral contract must be made to the offeror if the offeror might otherwise not have reason to know of the acceptance. This one sounds more complicated than it is. Recall that in a unilateral contract the offeror is seeking an act or performance, not just the promise to do the act called for in the contract. For example, Jane tells her teenage son John, "clean up your room and I'll let you use the car tonight." John cleans up his room while his mom is out grocery shopping. Jane has no way of knowing that her son John has cleaned up his room and is expecting to be allowed the car tonight. John needs to give his mother notice that he has performed his end of the agreement or bargain. John should call his mother and let her know or send her cellphone a picture of the now cleaned up room.

Method - The method for acceptance must be any reasonable mode of communication. An acceptance may be made in writing, verbally, via email, or fax. Some courts may find that a text/SMS suffices but it should be avoided until the law is settled on the matter. The contract offer may specify that acceptance may be made in a particular manner such as by mailing a signed copy of the contract offer United States Postal Service Express Delivery.

Act or Promise - A contract to do nothing at all is not a contract. A contract must be for some act or promise on the part of the offeree.

No Communication or Silence – A lack of response may not be construed as acceptance of the offer. Thus, stating to the offeree that if they do not reject the offer by a certain time period then the offer will be considered accepted will not obligate the offeree to perform the contract.

Remember, acceptance of an offer must be timely or acceptance will not be valid. <u>Late acceptance</u> or acceptance after a deadline has passed is not valid acceptance. In that situation, the offeror may treat the acceptance as a new offer which he or she may then reject.

Note that common law has said that verbal offers which are not accepted by the end of the conversation, without any other agreement for more time to think about the offer, are treated as rejected and the offer is terminated.

Terms

<u>Terms</u> vary enormously from contract to contract. No matter how complicated or industry-specific the subject matter is, terms should still be clearly written so that anyone reading the contract can understand what each party's obligations are. When reviewing the terms of a contract consider the following questions:

- Who is the agreement between and is there any transferability of rights?
- Who is providing any equipment/supplies for the performance?
- Where and when will the performance of the contract take place?
- Is there a penalty for not completing the project on time and who or what event determines that the contract has been completed?
- Where and when will payment be made? Will payments be made in installments?
- Are industry terms or commercial terms clearly understood to mean the same thing by both parties?
- Is there an inspection or quality review or other action by a 3rd party (such as a permit department) that needs to occur before the contract is concluded and payment can be made?

Answering these questions will help you determine what important clauses you need to include in the contract. Keep in mind that contracts are widely used legal instruments and there exists a plethora of resources to help you draft them. Contracts are seldom drafted from scratch. More often than not they are prepared with the help of form books, software templates, even similar documents from past cases. The caveat here is to thoroughly edit any boilerplate language to adapt the form to the specifics of the client's case. If you have any questions at all about boilerplate language you are using, check with your supervising attorney.

Consideration

<u>Consideration</u> is the price paid, the money exchanged or promise made that makes the contract happen. It is the secret sauce that makes the TACO come together. This is probably the area of contracts law to which most attention and care is given, but which probably generates the least amount of problems. Consideration is the name given to the price paid, the act requested to be

completed, and the promises exchanged. Consideration can be a promise to do something which the person would otherwise have no legal obligation to do. Thus, you don't see contracts which say, "I, Barbara, your mother, promise to care for you, my daughter, and shield you from illness and injury." A mother and father are legally required to care for and protect their children from harm. The promise not to do something must be in the nature of forbearance from doing something that the party would otherwise be allowed to do. For example, Uncle John makes an agreement with his nephew Larry that he will pay him $15.00/week for every week that Larry doesn't smoke cigarettes for the next six months. By the terms of the contract, Larry will refrain from smoking cigarettes even though he is over 18 and could otherwise purchase and smoke as many cigarettes as he likes. This example also illustrates that consideration doesn't have to be a benefit to the offeror, offeree, or either party at all.

Past consideration and gifts are not valid consideration for a contract and will make the contract unenforceable, if not void altogether. Past consideration describes a situation in which the actor or performance actually occurs *before* the promise of payment or consideration is made. For example, Lassie the dog saves you from drowning. You are so grateful you promise Timmy to build a brand new dog house for Lassie. It turns out you have post-traumatic stress disorder from your near drowning and never build the dog house for Lassie. Timmy has no cause of action for suing you because there was no contract between you and Timmy for the dog house. Past consideration is not actually any consideration at all and will not create a valid contract. Gifts are treated similarly and will not create a contract in which the recipient of the gift is obligated to give anything to the donor of the gift. When confusion arises, the key is to examine the motivation for any benefit received by the parties and its timing.

A contract which allows one party not to fulfill their obligation for no reason whatsoever or just "because they feel like it" is a contract with an illusory promise. This means the contract has no consideration and is not valid. Parties to a contract should each be making commitments and be bound by a duty to act in good faith.

When examining consideration take a close look at payment structures and whether partial or only complete payments may be made. Any language used must include terms, amount, time and place of payment, method, interest, as well as any partial or periodic payment plan.

> PAYMENT. Company will pay a fee to Contractor for the Services in the amount of $5,000.00. This fee shall be payable in a lump sum within 7 business days of completion of services.

FIGURE 12: Example compensation clause

Often, when consideration is made the ownership of something automatically changes hands. For example, if I sell my rug for $20 at a garage sale, I am no longer the owner of the rug. I have transferred ownership and control of the rug to a weekend bargain hunter in exchange for the agreed upon price of $20. Sometimes ownership does not change. Rather, the agreement grants the right to use a product for a certain amount of time and the original owner retains ownership. When you buy the latest software for your computer, a software ownership clause states that the software remains the property of the licensor. You have just purchased permission to use it.

A contract represents the agreements between two parties and the court cannot substitute a payment or punishment that was not contemplated by the parties. It is imperative that all terms and conditions are reviewed, researched and agreed upon prior to either party signing. A court will hesitate (absent extreme situations) to substitute its own judgment or price for the bargained-for exchange that was made in the contract and will not try to equalize or redefine the consideration.

EXECUTION

A process that paralegals are apt to be most closely involved with is the execution of the contract. <u>Execution</u> involves ensuring that all parties to the contract have completed the tasks which make the contract complete and enforceable. The first step is reviewing all required signatures. Signatures may be by authorized representatives of the company and/or legal representatives of a company. Any signatures should be followed by typed or printed names so that there is no confusion later about who signed the contract. Signature fields should also contain any titles or other language identifying the capacity of the person who has signed the contract. For example, a contract signature block may read "John Klein, President and Owner of HKL Plumbing Company".

Contracts are frequently dated and the date which appears should be the exact date on which the person actually signed the contract. Thus, date fields are frequently left blank until the person signing can fill it in. Some contracts require initials or initials and dates on all pages from one or all of the parties. It is the paralegal's duty to mark these spaces with tags before all parties meet and to review their completion after the parties have left the office. Frequently, there will be more than one original copy of a contract: one for filing in the attorney's office and one for each party to the contract. All original copies must be identical or disputes can arise later regarding whether or not all parties agreed to all terms.

Modern law practice means that a lot of electronic, faxed, and paper communication is sent back and forth. As such, the attorney counts on the paralegal to maintain the most accurate and recent version with edits. Some attorneys will even ask you to go back to prior versions of a contract to add back in a clause that had been removed! This is where attention to detail on the part of a paralegal is key. Without proper signatures, dates, copies, and attention to detail about when a contract's performance must begin, a contract may fail and become canceled or terminated for incomplete execution.

BREACH OF CONTRACT

A breach of contract may happen in several different ways. It can be a total breach or a partial breach. A breach may be a failure to perform some or all of the promises and duties described in the contract. Failure to perform is a breach, but so is preventing the ability of the other party to perform. For example, you agree to have Bugoff Exterminators come and tent your house for extermination on Friday. The day arrives and you are nowhere to be found, do not answer calls, and your Doberman is yipping at the exterminators' heels when they attempt to open your locked gate. Your actions prevented the performance of Bugoff Exterminators' duties and may be deemed to have breached the contract. The breach may be total or partial depending on whether the breach is material to the contract. Material is something that is significant or essential to the subject matter of the contract; something which if changed would have affected the decision making process of the contract.

If the breach is material, then the non-breaching party no longer owes any duty to perform or complete their own duties under the contract. If the breach is minor and thus not material then it may be considered only a partial breach and consideration must be paid for the performance rendered. For example, Bugoff Exterminators above manages to tent your entire house except for the homemade attached shed in the southeast corner because they did not know of its existence and do not have a tent large enough. You are still bound to pay Bugoff Exterminators for their work.

REMEDIES

So what happens if the contract is negotiated, signed, and there is still a breach? The law of remedies comes in to divide up the TACO. If there is a dispute as to whether or not the breach was material, the court will look at four elements:

1. hardship on the breaching party
2. amount of benefit the non-breaching party received
3. if the breach was purposeful, innocent, or accidental, and
4. if the non-breaching party can still do full or complete performance of their duties under the contract.

Substantial performance is a legal doctrine invoked where one party has mostly or substantially completed their duties under the contract. As high as 90% is sufficient, as low as 80% may not be enough, but a trivial or minor and inexpensive deficiency prevents performance from being

100%. One example might be you agree to have all new brushed nickel plumbing installed in your custom home. The plumber installed polished nickel plumbing instead. Polished nickel is a different look and finish and was not agreed to in the contract. Thus, performance or completion of the contract was not 100% exact. However, scientific studies show that polished nickel is just as effective as brushed nickel and discovery reveals that it would be prohibitively expensive for both you and the plumber to have the entire plumbing redone in the now mostly completed home. The court may rule that there was substantial performance completed and payment is owed to the plumber for his work. The court will order that consideration be paid despite the minor breach to prevent an injustice or unjust enrichment.

Unjust enrichment happens when one party receives part or all of a benefit under the contract and the party providing the benefit or performance receives no consideration. To promote fairness and to prevent an unfair precedent from occurring, the court may order a remedy of damages or payment in whole or in part. Unjust enrichment is often contemplated in personal service contracts. For example, you agree to have a stylist color, cut, and blow-dry your hair. The stylist spends 45 minutes coloring your hair, another 30 minutes cutting it, and then finishes blow-drying your hair in another 20 minutes. The stylist has now spent over an hour and half on services you requested. You suddenly decide you dislike the hair color you chose and will only pay for the cutting job. The stylist may choose to sue you for unjust enrichment for having received both her time and expertise in the performance of coloring and blow-drying your hair. Or in another example, ABC Developers contracts with Great Gardens Landscaping to complete all the basic landscaping for their next 25 homes. ABC Developers changes owners and becomes JKI Developers. In the process Great Gardens Landscaping never gets paid for their work, yet JKI manages to advertise all the homes with pictures of Great Gardens' landscaping and sells each house. Great Gardens may sue JKI for unjust enrichment since they received the benefit of advertising and selling homes with Great Gardens' work. An important factor the court examines with personal services and unjust enrichment claims is the fact that the work which was performed cannot be undone or could only be undone at great cost of even more time, expense, and labor. A landscaper cannot typically un-landscape a home or a stylist cannot uncut and un-color your hair.

Specific performance is a remedy that may be ordered by the court for a breach but it is actually very rare and only ordered when the subject of the contract is something unique, rare, or one of a kind. Contracts for the sale or leasing of land or homes often request specific performance because the law views every piece of land as unique and not capable of being duplicated. Specific performance will NOT be ordered in the case of personal services or musical performance contracts because of anti-slavery laws. For example, the court will not order a musician to sing in Central Park if she breaches a contract to perform a concert there, but the court may enjoin her from performing anywhere else.

Other types of remedies available for breaches of contract include money damages. Take care to look for and closely examine draft contracts for clauses that govern damages and remedies in the event of a breach. There is no such thing as recovering damages for pain and suffering or extreme emotional distress in contract law and such clauses inserted into contracts are likely to be severed per the severability clause. This is the case law precedent because a contract is merely a bargained for exchange of promises.

When it comes to damages decisions, courts aim to put the non-breaching or innocent party in the same position they would have been had the contract been performed or completed. If one party has partially performed or the other party has only partially paid the consideration then disputes arise. Part performance may be analyzed as well as the lost profit or bargain. Compensatory damages may be awarded to put the party in the position they would have been in *if the contract had been completed.* They are calculated by looking at expenses + profit loss/bargain loss. Foreseeability becomes an important concept. Only those expenses and losses that a reasonable person should or could have known would occur in the event of a breach will be contemplated.

Consequential or special damages may also be awarded if the natural and foreseeable consequences of the breach also resulted in a loss and the parties knew or had reason to know of this when they entered the contract. For example, Sally rents a car from ABC car rentals for a weekend road trip with her friends. On the day of their departure, ABC does not deliver the car preventing Sally from taking her road trip. Sally is unable to get any of her money back for the time share she rented for the weekend but was unable to get to as a result of ABC not performing.

Rescission is sometimes thought of as a pre-emptive remedy done by the innocent party after a breach. Rescission is the termination or cancellation of a contract after which the rescinding party attempts to obtain restitution for damages. If both parties agree to end a contract or terminate the old contract and enter into a new one it is called mutual rescission.

Instead of entering a new contract, parties to a contract may choose to reform it instead in a process called reformation. This is done when there is a math error, spelling, and phrasing or punctuation error or someone forgot to include a clause or term which they both did intend to include. Thus, a simple mistake was made not in the negotiation or contemplation of the contract but in the drafting and reducing it to writing. You can guess who will get the blame for this! Yet another reason proofreading is so important to the paralegal.

COMMON CONTENTS OF A CONTRACT

When drafting a contract, care must be taken to state all terms in clear, concise language that thoroughly communicates the intentions of the parties to the agreement. Each clause in a contract must be specifically tailored to the parties' needs. The following is a discussion of some common clauses found in contracts. It is in no way a complete list of possible clauses and it is not a list of required clauses. The order in which the clauses are presented are for instructional purposes only.

Every contract should begin with a title that clearly explains the nature of the document. I.e. "Pre-nuptial agreement", "Lease Agreement", or "Contract of Employment". This should be followed by an introductory paragraph that introduces the parties to the agreement, as well as the date of the agreement.

> THIS AGREEMENT, herein referred to as "Agreement", entered into this day, month, year constitutes an agreement by and between ABC Company, herein referred to as "Company", a Colorado corporation, having its principal office located at 123 Their Street, Anytown, CO, and Jane Doe, herein referred to as "Contractor", as follows:

FIGURE 13: Example beginning paragraph of contract, identifying the parties to a contract

Every contract should also include a statement of consideration after the party identification. For some contracts this may be sufficiently explained in a few sentences. The more likely circumstance is that the agreement has multiple points of consideration that need to be listed. In those instances, you may want to use something similar to the following:

> NOW, THEREFORE, in consideration of the premises and mutual covenants hereinafter contained, the parties agree as follows:

FIGURE 14: Example consideration clause

You would need to follow this preamble with a complete list of all items in consideration for the agreement.

Most contracts will be for a specified period of time. The "Term" or "Termination of Agreement" clause includes specifications regarding the termination of the agreement and any stipulations regarding notification of termination. Automatic renewal options may also be included in this section for long-term agreements.

> TERM. This agreement shall have an initial term of five (5) years, calculated from the date the agreement is signed by both parties. This term shall be automatically renewed for subsequent two-year terms, unless notice of termination in writing is given by one party to the other no fewer than two (2) months prior to the expiration of the initial term or any subsequent term.

FIGURE 15: Example termination of agreement clause.

The <u>definitions clause</u> of a contract is where both parties want to clearly define any industry specific terms or really any terms that may be questionable later on as to what they cover. A common place most of us have seen these types of definitions is a homeowners' insurance policy. This may not register right away as a contract but any policy is in effect a contract between you and the policy provider.

<u>DEFINITIONS.</u>   For the purposes of this Agreement, the meaning accorded terminology used herein shall be as follows:

"Jewelry" means individually owned objects of personal decoration comprised partially of platinum, gold, silver, or other precious metals or alloys, whether or not containing pearls, jewels, or precious or semi-precious stones.

"Fur" means furs and attire trimmed with animal fur.

"Cameras" means cameras, projection machines and miscellaneous property such as carrying cases, filters, lenses, films, tripods, light meters, etc.

FIGURE 16: Example Definitions clause

When evaluating any contract seek out the <u>merger clause</u>. This is frequently, though not always, included and has been called by various terms including entire agreement, entirety of agreement, complete agreement, etc. This clause will specifically state that the four corners of the contract will govern the agreement between the parties and all prior draft agreements, notes on negotiations, communications, conversations and the like have either been voided by the contract or been merged into and incorporated into the contract. This merger clause will make a contract an <u>integrated contract</u>, meaning that the contract contains the entire agreement among the parties involved.

<u>MERGER CLAUSE:</u> This Agreement represents the entire agreement between Company and Contractor with respect to the subject matter of this Agreement and supersedes all prior oral and written arrangements, negotiations and agreements between the parties.

FIGURE 17: Example merger clause

The <u>severability clause</u> frequently found in contracts states that if any provision or part of the contract is found to be illegal or unenforceable then the offending clause will be deleted and the rest of the contract will remain enforceable.

SEVERABILITY OF CLAUSES: In the event that any provision or portion of this Agreement shall be held to be invalid, illegal, unenforceable or in conflict with the law of any jurisdiction, in whole or in part, such provision shall be of no force and effect, and all remaining provisions of this Contract agreement shall be unaffected thereby.

FIGURE 18: Example severability clause

Contracts may contain a transfer/assignability of rights clause so that the rights are or are not assignable to any third party. For example, you enter into an agreement for a custom made hot rod car with Extreme Designs, Inc. Unfortunately halfway to completion of the hot rod, you are asked to immediately deploy to Jordan for two years. Rather than lose your deposit and waste the time spent consulting with and designing your hot rod with Extreme Designs, Inc. you convince your brother-in-law he would like to take over the hot rod contract and finish the project for himself. Your contract with Extreme Designs, Inc. may allow you to transfer the rights and benefits of your deposits, design choices thus far, and the benefits of any discounts you negotiated to your brother in law. The contract may or may not explicitly state that Extreme Designs, Inc. has the right to object to this arrangement with your brother-in-law. In this arrangement, there is no new contract. Rather the same contract between yourself and Extreme Designs, Inc. continues with your rights and benefits under the contract having been transferred and assigned instead to your brother-in-law.

ASSIGNABILITY. The warranties, representations, agreements, and covenants contained in this Agreement are for the sole benefit of the parties hereto and shall not be construed as conferring any rights on any other persons or entities.

FIGURE 19: Example assignability of rights clause

You may see a liquidated damages clause which attempts to fix a certain amount that will be paid if one of the parties cannot fulfill its promise and duty under the contract. Frequently, parties will try to limit or change the available remedies and damages traditionally available in case of a breach. Liquidated damages are meant to be a reasonable estimate of loss the parties believe may occur because the true estimate is too difficult or impossible to calculate. The amount cannot be so unreasonable or so grossly out of proportion to the value of the contract and the facts and circumstances that it acts as a punishment. How does the court determine if the liquidated damages clause is reasonable and not punitive? The reasonableness of the amount will be determined by examining evidence of the statements and intentions of the parties *at the time they agreed to the contract.* If the liquidated damages clause is activated two years after the contract was signed the court will not examine whether or not the clause now seems grossly inflated and feels like a penalty. The court will examine what was contemplated at the time the contract was signed. For example, a sculptor receives his first commission for making a public art piece for the newest museum in town. Sculptor's agent negotiates a $50,000 liquidated damages clause if museum decides they don't like his finished piece and won't use it thereby denying sculptor of the public acclaim he expected to receive beyond mere payment for the work. The museum agrees to this clause because they have $10,000,000 in bonds and figure they won't breach the contract. The economy does not do well and the bonds fall in value. The museum is not built and Sculptor sues. The museum is unlikely to successfully argue that $50,000 is a punishment to pay because at the time they negotiated and agreed to the contract and its liquidated damages clause they believed the $50,000 to be a reasonable amount.

LIQUIDATED DAMAGES. Guests canceling their reservation after occupying unit shall pay liquidated damages in the amount of $50.00 per day for the remainder or unexpired portion of the term of reservation, not to exceed $500.00.

FIGURE 20: Example liquidated damages clause

Exculpatory damages clause holds one party free from blame and relieves them of any liability for damage caused in the execution of a contract. You may have seen this at the dry cleaner when they say they are not responsible for damage caused to your clothing due to machine malfunction or chemical accident.

EXCLUSIONS. This Agreement does not cover loss or damage to property caused by wear and tear, gradual deterioration, or inherent vice.

FIGURE 21: Example exclusions clause

The case law, applicable law or governing law clause will identify the body of law to be applied in the event of a dispute. The choice is most often based on the residence of one or both parties. This clause is included to stipulate the jurisdiction of a particular court.

GOVERNING LAW. This Agreement shall be governed by the laws of the State of Colorado applicable to agreements made and to be performed within such State. The parties agree that the state and federal courts located in Colorado shall have exclusive jurisdiction over any claims arising out of this Agreement.

FIGURE 22: Example applicable law

Some contracts may call for a release of liability/indemnification clause. Releases from liability are typically encountered in recreational activities. For example, when taking tennis lessons from a gym you may be asked to sign a release which states that you will not sue the tennis instructor or facility for any injuries incurred while learning to play. Indemnification clauses are very similar but have a slightly different focus. Indemnification would take the form of agreeing to hold the tennis instructor and tennis facility blameless and free from responsibility or liability for any harm caused by you twisting your ankle while taking tennis lessons. The focus in a release is on you giving up a right you would normally have. In an indemnification you agree that the tennis instructor or facility will not be held liable for damages caused by your twisted ankle which are claimed by third parties. Beware of release and indemnification clauses which are so overly broad as to go beyond what is allowed by state law. Most states will rule releases which aim to protect a party from damages caused by intentional or reckless wrongdoing to be void as against public policy.

> WARRANTIES AND INDEMNITIES. Contractor shall hold harmless, defend, and indemnify Company, its officers, employees, and representatives from and against all liability, loss, costs, and/or obligations on account of or arising from Contractor's negligent acts and omissions, willful or intentional acts, and for any and all liability arising out of Contractor's breach of any representation or warranty set forth in this Agreement.

FIGURE 23: Example warranties and indemnities clause

The modification clause is included in most contracts to prohibit and/or limit any changes made to the agreement.

> MODIFICATION. This Agreement may not be modified or amended except by a further written instrument or by an amendment to this Agreement signed by Contractor and Company.

FIGURE 24: Example modification clause

The arbitration clause or disputes clause, as it is sometimes called, outlines the preferred method for dispute resolutions. Parties can stipulate that mediation, arbitration or other dispute resolutions methods be applied prior to resorting to litigation.

> DISPUTES. Contractor and Company agree to attempt to resolve disputes arising from this agreement by administrative process and negotiation in lieu of litigation. In the event of a dispute between Contractor and Company over any part of this Agreement, the dispute may be submitted to non-binding arbitration upon the consent of both parties. An election for arbitration pursuant to this provision shall not preclude either party from pursuing any remedy for relief otherwise available.

FIGURE 25: Example arbitration clause

There may also be an attorney fees clause which may or may not be combined with a litigation costs clause. These clauses outlines liability for attorney and litigation costs should a dispute not be resolved through arbitration.

ATTORNEY FEES. In the event of the employment by the Company of any attorney to collect services due or to protect the interest of any of the terms and conditions of the Agreement, Contractor will pay to Company the reasonable fees of such attorney and such fee shall be forthwith due and payable upon demand.

FIGURE 26: Example attorney fees clause

LITIGATION COSTS. If any action at Law shall be brought on account of any breach of, or to enforce or interpret any of the covenants, terms and conditions of this agreement, the prevailing party shall be entitled to any and all costs incurred in connection with such action, and any and all reasonable attorney's fees, the amount of which shall be fixed by the court, and shall be made a part of any judgment or decree rendered.

FIGURE 27: Example litigation costs clause

The contract may also contain language outlining terms for one or more parties to terminate the agreement.

Company reserves the right to terminate this Agreement immediately and without charge or penalty under any of the following circumstances:

FIGURE 28: Example termination clause

The all-important meeting of the minds concept comes into play when examining terms. Do both parties understand and think of the same thing when they are agreeing to this contract? Both parties should intend to be bound by the promises made in the contract. If a dispute arises and a court has to make a decision they will do so according to the objective reasonable person standard. If the court cannot determine what a reasonable person would believe the terms to be, the court can declare there is no contract.

Believe it or not there is a famous contracts case which turned on the definition of the word chicken! One party intended to purchase fresh, young chickens suitable for broiling and roasting and the other party, the seller, believed older chickens suitable for stewing satisfied the contract. The court ultimately ruled that any reasonable person, including any person in the chicken industry, could have believed either type of chicken sufficed so there was no contract due to <u>mutual mistake</u>. *Frigalimeat Import Co. v. BNS Int'l Sales Corp.*, 190 F. Supp. 116 (S.D.N.Y. 1960).

Conclusion

Contracts can seem daunting at first. They have multiple pages, tiny writing, and can be difficult to follow. The trick to evaluating a contract is to break out each section and examine it separately. Do not get frustrated by some of the boilerplate language used for different clauses. Over time you will learn to zero in on the key details that matter to your firm's clients or to your own interests. When evaluating a contract, ask the following:

- What is the client being asked to do?
- When is the client supposed to finish?
- What happens if your law firm's client doesn't complete the contract?
- How much will the client be paid and when?
- Is the client relying on an event or person to help complete this contract but who is not mentioned in this contract?

If you can answer these simple questions, then you will be able to adequately summarize and discuss contract terms knowledgeably and become a valued member of your legal team.

Chapter Three: Federal & State Pleadings

Jolie R. Kulsar

As you know, civil litigation arises from instances in which a person, group of people, or a business entity feels they have been harmed by another. The party initiating the lawsuit is known as the plaintiff whereas the party accused of causing the harm is known as the defendant. Once the attorney-client relationship has been formalized through the retainer agreement, the plaintiff's attorney notifies the defendant of the damages sustained by the plaintiff through the demand letter. The demand letter provides the defendant with a specified period of time in which to provide restitution. Should the defendant fail to respond, or refuse to settle, the parties must then prepare for trial and the preparation and filing of numerous legal documents, including pleadings and motions.

The documents filed by the plaintiff to commence a lawsuit and the documents filed by the defendant in response to the lawsuit are called pleadings. The Federal Rules of Civil Procedure govern pleading construction and procedures in the federal courts and state civil rules govern pleading at the state level.

TYPES & PURPOSE OF PLEADINGS

Complaint

A civil action is commenced by filing a complaint with the court. (FRCP 3) Sometimes referred to as the petition, the complaint is the document by which the plaintiff initiates the lawsuit and informs the defendant of the basis for the claim. It is the first document that will be seen by the defendant, opposing counsel and the court, and will be referenced repeatedly as the case proceeds.

Summons

While not, strictly speaking, a pleading, the summons is served along with the complaint and is an important and required step in initiating an action. The summons notifies the defendant that a lawsuit has been filed against him and that a response is required. In some jurisdictions the summons is prepared by the court clerk. In others, it is prepared by the plaintiff's attorney along with the complaint, and presented to the clerk at the time the complaint is filed.

Responsive Pleadings

After the defendant is served with the summons and complaint, they typically have 20 - 30 days in which to file a response. If the defendant does not file a response within the required time period, the plaintiff can request that the court award a default judgment. The defendant's response can take several forms:

The Answer to the Complaint must admit, deny, or claim a lack of knowledge with regard to each allegation set forth in the body of the complaint. The defendant may admit to the allegations in some paragraphs, claim a lack of knowledge regarding the accuracy of other paragraphs, and deny allegations set forth in other paragraphs depending on the circumstances. In most courts, any paragraph in the complaint which contains allegations can be admitted in part and denied in part, but any allegations that are not specifically denied are deemed admitted.

The defendant may allege **affirmative defenses** which argue that, even if the plaintiff's claims are true, facts exist which serve to mitigate or diminish liability. If affirmative defenses are asserted in the defendant's answer, the plaintiff must then file a Reply to Affirmative Defenses either admitting or denying the facts asserted therein. Affirmative defenses are typically set forth within the body of the answer.

A counter-claim is a demand for relief made by a defendant in a civil case against a plaintiff, asserting that the defendant is entitled to damages of their own. As with the counts charged in the plaintiff's complaint, the counterclaim must allege the facts, harm incurred, and liability of the plaintiff, and request relief for damages. The plaintiff must then file an answer to those allegations. Counter-claims may be allowed even if their nature or subject matter is completely unrelated to the original claim. A counter-claim may be included as part of the defendant's answer or prepared as a separate document.

Cross-claims are filed between parties on the same side of the original case. Once the original complaint is filed, a plaintiff who has a dispute with another plaintiff, or a defendant who has a dispute with another defendant, may choose to file a cross-claim against that other person. Unlike counter-claims which can be based on any legal dispute the defendant has against the plaintiff, the issues in the cross-claim must be based on the same basic facts that are involved either in the original case or in a counter-claim filed in the original case.

A third-party complaint is filed against a defendant who has not already been named as a party to the suit. Third party complaints can be filed by the plaintiff or the defendant and allege that the third party is, in some way, responsible for the damages sought. The third party generally has a right to defend against the claim, including raising any defenses against the plaintiff or the defendant, which may apply.

Responsive pleadings follow the form of the complaint and, at the time of filing with the court clerk, copies must be mailed or delivered to counsel for each party to the claim. Some responsive pleadings may require further replies from the opposing party. For instance, a third-party complaint requires an answer from the third-party defendant, a counterclaim may require a reply from the plaintiff, or a court may allow a reply to an answer.

The documents listed above are formally categorized as pleadings. Below some examples of motions and other documents that may also be filed during the early stages of litigation.

A **motion to dismiss** is a legal document that asks the court to "throw out" a case for factual defects or procedural errors. The motion is usually filed by the defendant immediately after the plaintiff files a complaint. A defendant can file a motion to dismiss instead of filing an answer, as courts assume the defendant denies the allegations in the complaint, even though the defendant hasn't filed an answer specifically denying them.

A **demurrer** is a response to the complaint which asserts that even if the facts presented are true, they are not enough to prove the defendant is legally responsible or liable for any damages. The complaint must fully allege each element (conditions which must be present) of the claim. If the facts provided do not fully support the elements, the claim will be unsuccessful. In federal courts, as well as the majority of states, the demurrer has been replaced with the motion to dismiss for failure to state a claim upon which relief can be granted, or failure to state facts sufficient to support a cause of action.

A **pretrial motion** is a written request to the court asking the judge to take some action in the matter. Because motions usually involve questions of law or legal procedure, they are generally signed by the attorney rather than the client and argued by the attorney at a hearing. Pre-trial motions including the motion to dismiss will be discussed later in this chapter.

Other documents which may be prepared when filing pleadings and motions include, but are not limited to, affidavits, verifications, orders, notices and notary public acknowledgments.

Affidavits are written statements of facts made under oath before an office of the court or a notary public. Motions relying on facts not contained in an exhibit must include an affidavit sworn to by the client, witness or party offering the information. An attorney affidavit is frequently provided in support of a motion, or when the attorney has reason to assert facts or relevant factual background. Information regarding an oversight or error on the attorney's part, for instance, would be prepared as an affidavit.

A verification is a declaration under oath or upon penalty of perjury attesting to the truth of the statements within a document. Unless required by statute or rule, pleadings do not necessarily need to be verified, as the attorney's signature basically attests to the veracity of the assertions set forth therein. When required, the verification is generally by affidavit. When a verified complaint is served, it is important that the answer to the complaint be verified, as well. Notarization is not required by the federal courts, but pleadings filed in state courts will frequently be notarized.

Court orders reflect the judge's ruling on a motion. When the motion and exhibits are filed, the attorney generally prepares a proposed order reflecting the relief sought through the motion. The court's ruling on the issues is then provided along with the location of the court (county/state, etc) and a signature line is prepared indicating the name and title below the line. A date line is also included.

Notices advise other parties/counsel of hearings, depositions or other events related to the case. Notices are formatted to include the caption, the purpose of the notice including any pertinent information, such as a hearing time, date and location, the signature block of the attorney and a certificate of service.

Some documents filed with the court must be notarized. A ***notary public acknowledgment*** attests to and certifies the genuineness of the legal instrument. A notary public is appointed by the state to administer oaths and take acknowledgments. The notary signs and dates a statement indicating that the person whose signature must be notarized has appeared and proven their identity. The attorney preparing the document to be notarized includes the acknowledgment below the signature, on the same page or immediately following, and appears as below.

Finally, some motions rely on information not contained within the complaint. If the moving party wishes the judge to consider additional facts, documents, deposition testimony or other forms of evidence not alleged in the complaint, the materials are attached to the complaint as exhibits. There are many other motions which might be filed throughout litigation. While content and purpose varies from motion to motion, the general components remain fairly consistent. As always, check your rules of court for specific filing and format requirements.

CONSTRUCTION OF PLEADINGS

It is important that your pleadings conform to your court rules, and that they be accurate and substantive enough to overcome any challenges due to insufficient information, allegations or assertions. The facts upon which a claim is based are crucial to success or failure and lawsuits can fail due to being weakly pled. While specific requirements can vary significantly from court to court, keep the following general considerations in mind when drafting your pleadings:

- Pleadings must establish the legal issues of the case. Limit allegations to statements of fact that are relevant to the claim:

- A material allegation in a pleading is one essential to the claim or defense, and which could not be stricken from the pleading without leaving it insufficient.
- Legal arguments and legal authority are normally included in motions, but not in pleadings.
- Avoid references to evidence with the exception of documents relied upon to support factual allegations. Follow directions when submitting any permitted exhibits with pleadings.

- Pleadings should be relevant, on point and coherent; focus and attention to detail is important:
  - State material facts that form the basis of the claim.
  - Set forth each allegation as its own paragraph.
  - Provide enough detail to explain the nature of the allegation.
  - Do not raise facts that are not directly pertinent to the current allegation.
  - Ensure that the name of the court and the parties are correct.
  - Use full names for individuals and the registered name of any corporation.

- Number paragraphs for easy reference
  - Each allegation should be set forth in a separate and distinct numbered paragraph.
  - Remember that replies will address each assertion on a point by point basis. Numbered paragraphs provide for ease of reference and location. Remember this when drafting a reply as well.

- Use professional language, prepare drafts, proofread carefully.
  - Remember that you are writing for the court. Avoid slang and sarcasm, use professional tone, and keep language simple and clearly written.
  - Thoroughly check for spelling and grammar issues prior to finalizing.

The form of pleadings and other court documents filed in the federal courts is set forth in the Federal Rules of Civil Procedure. The general components of most pleadings include the caption, the title, the body, the prayer for relief, the signature block and, for all pleadings filed after the initial complaint, a certificate of service or mailing.

Rule 8 of the Federal Rules of Civil Procedure reads, in part, as follows:

General Rules of Pleading

(a) ___Claim for Relief.___ *A pleading that states a claim for relief must contain:*

(1) a short and plain statement of the grounds for the court's jurisdiction, unless the court already has jurisdiction and the claim needs no new jurisdictional support;

(2) a short and plain statement of the claim showing that the pleader is entitled to relief; and

(3) a demand for the relief sought, which may include relief in the alternative or different types of relief.

(b) ___Defenses;___ *Admissions and Denials.*

(1) In General. In responding to a pleading, a party must:

(A) state in short and plain terms its defenses to each claim asserted against it; and

(B) admit or deny the allegations asserted against it by an opposing party.

(2) Denials—Responding to the Substance. A denial must fairly respond to the substance of the allegation.

(3) General and Specific Denials. A party that intends in good faith to deny all the allegations of a pleading— including the jurisdictional grounds—may do so by a general denial. A party that does not intend to deny all the allegations must either specifically deny designated allegations or generally deny all except those specifically admitted.

(4) Denying Part of an Allegation. A party that intends in good faith to deny only part of an allegation must admit the part that is true and deny the rest.

(5) Lacking Knowledge or Information. A party that lacks knowledge or information sufficient to form a belief about the truth of an allegation must so state, and the statement has the effect of a denial.

(6) Effect of Failing to Deny. An allegation—other than one relating to the amount of damages—is admitted if a responsive pleading is required and the allegation is not denied. If a responsive pleading is not required, an allegation is considered denied or avoided.

(d) Pleading to Be Concise and Direct; Alternative Statements; Inconsistency.

(1) In General. Each allegation must be simple, concise, and direct. No technical form is required.

(2) Alternative Statements of a Claim or Defense. A party may set out 2 or more statements of a claim or defense alternatively or hypothetically, either in a single count or defense or in separate ones. If a party makes alternative statements, the pleading is sufficient if any one of them is sufficient.

(3) Inconsistent Claims or Defenses. A party may state as many separate claims or defenses as it has, regardless of consistency.

(e) Construing Pleadings. Pleadings must be construed so as to do justice.

While pursuant to FRCP 10:

(a) Caption; Names of Parties. Every pleading must have a caption with the court's name, a title, a file number, and a Rule 7(a) designation. The title of the complaint must name all the parties; the title of other pleadings, after naming the first party on each side, may refer generally to other parties.

(b) Paragraphs; Separate Statements. A party must state its claims or defenses in numbered paragraphs, each limited as far as practicable to a single set of circumstances. A later pleading may refer by number to a paragraph in an earlier pleading. If doing so would promote clarity, each claim founded on a separate transaction or occurrence—and each defense other than a denial—must be stated in a separate count or defense.

Specific formatting preferences, however, such as proper identification of the judge, inclusion of a case cover sheet, typeface, margins or citation preferences, for example, vary by court. Therefore, it is important that you always check your local rules of court for specific guidelines. The local rules from two different US District Courts provided on the following pages clearly illustrate this point.

United States District Court for the Eastern District Of California	
LOCAL RULES: **Rule 130 General Format of Documents**	*(b) Conventionally-Filed Documents and Courtesy Copies. All documents presented for conventional filing or lodging and the chambers courtesy copies shall be on white, unglazed opaque paper of good quality with numbered lines in the left margin, 8-1/2" x 11" in size, and shall be flat, unfolded (except where necessary for presentation of exhibits), firmly bound at the top left corner, pre-punched with two (2) holes (approximately 1/4" diameter) centered 2-3/4" apart, 1/2" to 5/8" from the top edge of the document, and shall comply with all other applicable provisions of these Rules.* *Matters contained thereon shall be presented by typewriting, printing, photographic or offset reproduction, or other clearly legible process, without erasures or interlining that materially defaces the document, and shall appear on one side of each sheet only.* *(c) Spacing. Documents shall be double-spaced except for the identification of counsel, title of the action, category headings, footnotes, quotations, exhibits and descriptions of real property. Quotations of more than fifty (50) words shall be indented.* *(d) Numbering. Each page shall be numbered consecutively at the bottom and shall provide a brief description of the document on the same line.*

United States District Court Southern District of New York	
Local Civil Rule **11.1. Form of Pleadings, Motions, and Other Papers**	*(a) Every pleading, written motion, and other paper must* *(1) be plainly written, typed, printed, or copied without erasures or interlineations which materially deface it,* *(2) bear the docket number and the initials of the District Judge and any Magistrate Judge before whom the action or proceeding is pending, and* *(3) have the name of each person signing it clearly printed or typed directly below the signature.* *(b) The typeface, margins, and spacing of all documents presented for filing must meet the following requirements:* *(1) all text must be 12-point type or larger, except for text in footnotes which may be 10-point type;* *(2) all documents must have at least one -inch margins on all sides;* *(3) all text must be double-spaced, except for headings, text in footnotes, or block quotations, which may be single-spaced.*

General Format

Failure to follow specifications set forth in your rules of court can result in the court's refusal to accept the document for filing. Most offices create and maintain a directory of forms or templates that have been pre-formatted according to the rules of the courts in which the attorneys most frequently appear. However, be prepared to consult local rules of court (or a helpful court clerk) when any doubt exists, or if the office has not automated these procedures. Remember that these rules are updated from time to time, so it is important to remain current through published rules, CLE seminars, state bar publications, etc.

Caption

The caption is the formal heading of a legal document appearing at the top of the page and includes the name of the court in which the case will be filed, the names and designation of the parties involved in the matter and the case number. In addition, many courts require that the attorney representing the party be identified.

- o **Name of Court**
  - o Verify and enter the complete court name
  - o The official name is normally centered or aligned with the left margin as the court's rules dictate
  - o Generally keyed in all caps

- o **Docket number**
  - o Docket number is left blank when preparing the complaint until it has been assigned by the court when the complaint is filed
  - o For complaints filed in person, the court clerk will enter the docket number.
  - o If the complaint is filed electronically, the system will generate and enter it automatically
  - o The docket number must appear on all subsequent documents
  - o The Docket number is provided to the right of the party names
  - o Generally keyed in all caps

- o **Title of the action**
  - o Identify the full name and status of all parties to the case
    - In matters involving multiple plaintiffs or multiple defendants, all parties must be named on the complaint pursuant to FRCP 10(a). In all other documents, only the name of the first party is required, followed by "et al."
    - Corporations are generally identified by the corporate name, Example: *AAA Automotive, a New York Corporation*
    - Public officers sued in their official capacity are generally identified by official title, though the court may order that the officer's given name be added. (FRCP 17(d)).
  - o Specify the party's role at trial (Plaintiff or Defendant); always enter the plaintiff first.
  - o Parties are entered on the left margin below the court name with the plaintiff entered first, followed on the next line by "v" (abbreviation for versus) and then the defendant
  - o Generally keyed in all caps

- o **Document title** (e.g. "Complaint"; "Defendant's Answer to Complaint" etc.)
  - o Enter the title under the docket number.
  - o Federal courts generally require that the nature of the claim be included in the title. Example: Complaint for Negligence.
  - o Federal courts generally require that a Demand for Jury Trial be entered below the document title

---

IN THE UNITED STATES DISTRICT COURT
FOR THE

EASTERN DISTRICT OF NEW YORK

SANFORD & SONS LIMITED,
a Swiss Corporation,

                                   Plaintiff,   **NO.** _____

v.

CAC AVIATION CORPORATION
a New York Corporation,

                                   Defendant.

COMPLAINT FOR BREACH OF CONTRACT,
UNJUST ENRICHMENT, AND CONVERSION
WITH JURY TRIAL

FIGURE 29: Example Federal Court Caption

NOTE: See Figures 2 & 3 in Chapter One for example state court captions.

Paper Size and Margins

Generally pleadings must be written on 8.5 inch by 11 inch pre-numbered pleading paper which can be easily created using pleadings templates in MS Word, Open Office and other word processing programs. In all likelihood, your office will already have templates for most of your pleadings, motions and discovery documents and formatted according the rules of the court or courts in which your attorney most commonly appears.

Most local court rules will specify either 12 or 14-pt font size with 1 inch margins on all sides unless the court requires a case cover sheet, in which case, the top margin preference is generally 2 1/4 inches, however, this is not the case when pleadings are filed electronically. Many courts will also specify the preferred font-type.

Signatures

The attorney's signature block should include the name, address and telephone number of the attorney providing representation. Some jurisdictions also require the attorney's state bar ID number. The law firm and identification of the party represented is generally provided above the signature line, but this may vary based on court and/or attorney preference. *See Figure 10 in Chapter One for an example attorney signature block.*

Body of pleadings

The body or text of most court documents states facts, sets forth specific allegations, or makes requests through separate numbered paragraphs, to which the opposing party may easily and directly respond. Depending on the court, additional headings might include statements of jurisdiction or venue, party information, the prayer for relief and jury demands where required and applicable.

The body is generally double-spaced and begins with a preamble, which introduces the party and the purpose of the document. Frequently, the text of the first word is entered in bold-faced type and may be indented; if the pleading includes subheadings, such as different causes of action, the title of each heading is capitalized, underlined and entered in bold-faced type, so that they are easily identifiable.

See Figure 6 in Chapter One for an example introductory preamble for a complaint. See Figure 8 in Chapter One for an example of the body of a complaint.

Forms

The preparation of pleadings and motions can be a time consuming task requiring thought, analysis and attention to detail. An improperly drafted pleading can be rejected by the court, or even be grounds for dismissal of the case. Standardized sample documents, or forms, allow us to avoid repeatedly starting from scratch. Some forms are simple, fill-in-the-blank-type replicas similar to word processing templates. Others include annotations to explain the necessary elements as well as ensure that the document is drafted to include them.

Bound collections of legal forms, or form books, have removable sample forms to assist in document preparation. These collections may serve as general forms collections and may be organized by practice area, subject matter or jurisdiction. Books for practice in a given state may be published by state courts, state bar associations or private publishers, and civil procedure rule books usually include sample forms in the appendices.

Pleadings and practice forms contain the suggested terminology, formatting and elements essential to a cause of action and provide the language and formatting required for the document. Many form books include alternate forms and/or optional clauses that can be added to customize the basic form to suit the legal matter. In addition, they may include helpful checklists, annotations, and cross-references to other publications and features. Some of the more commonly used pleadings-related form books include:

- o *Am. Jur. Proof of Facts* – used to ensure that the facts alleged support the cause of action

- o *Am. Jur. Trials* – assists in developing trial strategy

- o *Am. Jur. Pleading and Practice Forms* -- a general template-style form book

- o *Causes of Action* -- addresses elements involved in a specific cause of action and the allegations that must be alleged to fully establish the claim

- o *West's Federal Forms* -- an annotated general form book for matters filed in federal court.

Books are no longer the only source of legal forms. Most courts now provide at least some of their forms online. In fact, court websites are quickly becoming the first stop in shopping for forms, as the number of *pro se* litigants continues to increase. Nearly all offices maintain a forms file or database, and the selection of software programs to suit this need will certainly increase, and advance in features.

It is important to note, however, that standardized forms must be treated as examples and will need to be refined or modified to suit the specific legal matter. Forms should be used as a starting place and then tailored to reflect the matter at hand. Laws and court rules are constantly changing so, when using a form, it is necessary to ensure that the form is current, that you have read it carefully, and that you have revised it as needed.

PREPARING A COMPLAINT FOR A FEDERAL CASE

Under FRCP 3, a civil action is commenced by filing a complaint with the court. Sometimes referred to as the petition, the complaint is the document by which the plaintiff initiates the lawsuit. The complaint serves to notify the defendant that a claim has been filed and to set forth the basis of the claim for both the defendant and the court. While the length of this document will vary based on the complexity of the case, as the first document filed in the legal matter, it is important that it be prepared accurately.

A properly drafted complaint clearly indicates that the plaintiff has been harmed, that the basis of the claim is legitimate, and that the claim for relief is justified. In order to accomplish this, it is important to research the facts, claims, arguments and counter-arguments surrounding your cause of action, as well as relevant law and procedural rules.

Checklist

Once the attorney has evaluated the facts and issues upon which the claim is based, the process of preparing the lawsuit begins. This process generally involves a variety of tasks including legal investigation and fact gathering, legal research, interviewing and administrative duties. Prior to commencing litigation, the following should be completed:

- Ensure that no conflict of interest exists by running a conflict check
- Execute the retainer agreement
- Identify and calendar the statute of limitations
- Open and continually build the litigation file for the claim
- Evaluate the merits of the plaintiff's claims
- Meet with the client to review the facts and key documents
- Investigate the facts of the dispute to determine validity of all claims
- Identify damages and relief sought by the plaintiff
- Determine proper jurisdiction and venue
- Identify the elements necessary to the claim
- Review related statutes, case law & substantive and procedural rules
- Research and evaluate defendant's potential defenses to the claims
- Determine evidence required to prove the claim
- Investigate key documents including:

- location
- burden and expense of collection and production
- relevant documents which serve to substantiate the claim
- admissibility of documents
- existence of documents damaging to the claim
  - o Identify the relevant witnesses, including:
    - credibility
    - cooperative or hostile witness
    - subject to the court's jurisdiction
    - potential of and need for expert witnesses
  - o Issue a litigation hold or preservation letter instructing the defendant to cease any and all activity which may result in the destruction or modification of relevant files, including those maintained electronically.

Substance of the complaint

The complaint may be drafted once the necessary investigation, research and administrative tasks have been undertaken, and the validity of the claim has been established. Again, it is important that you consult the FRCP, as well as the rules of court in which the claim will be filed before you begin. These specify substantive content requirements, proper formatting, and other required documents, such as the summons, and filing and service requirements. Pleadings not conforming to those provisions may be rejected by the court.

The complaint generally consists of the caption; the body, the signature, and the demand for jury trial where desired.

Identify parties

This section introduces the parties to the court. The plaintiff is identified first, and in such a way which clarifies their standing and the relief sought. When introducing the defendant, the injuries sustained by the plaintiff should be named, as well as the role the defendant played in inflicting those injuries. However, the primary purpose of this section is to support the assertions to be set forth in the Statement of Jurisdiction and to establish the party's capacity to sue and be sued.

The plaintiff must have legal capacity to bring the lawsuit. In federal courts, the capacity of an individual to sue or be sued is generally determined by state law. For example, many states have laws stipulating that partnerships and unincorporated voluntary associations have the capacity to sue or be sued. Legal capacity is determined as follows:

- o For an individual, by the law of her domicile
- o For a corporation, by the law of its state of incorporation
- o For all other parties, by the law of the state where the court is located, except that:

- a partnership or other unincorporated association with no legal capacity under that state's law may sue or be sued in its common name to enforce a substantive right existing under US law; and
- the capacity of a receiver appointed by a US court to sue or be sued in a US court is governed by 28 U.S.C. §§ 754 and 959(a).

If a person lacks the capacity to sue by reason of infancy or incompetence, the court may appoint a guardian as the person's representative (FRCP 17(c)).

Jurisdiction & Venue

The Statement of Jurisdiction fulfills the plaintiff's burden of proving that the court has jurisdiction over the case. A complaint filed in federal courts must include a "short and plain statement of the grounds for the court's jurisdiction" (FRCP 8). As you will recall from prior lessons, the federal courts have jurisdiction over disputes involving federal law (federal question jurisdiction under 28 U.S.C. §1331) or when the parties involved are citizens of different states and the amount in controversy exceeds $75,000 (diversity jurisdiction 28 U.S.C. §1332(a)). A complaint based on diversity jurisdiction must identify the citizenship of all parties and state that the amount in controversy exceeds $75,000.

In matters involving parties other than individuals, for jurisdiction purposes, a corporation is considered a citizen of (1) every domestic state in which it is incorporated, (2) every foreign state in which it is incorporated, and (3) any state, domestic or foreign, in which its principal place of business exists. Unincorporated entities, such as a limited liability company or partnership, are considered citizens of all states wherein each member or partner is a citizen. The principal place of business, however, does not determine residency if the entity is unincorporated.

Apart from and in addition to personal and subject matter jurisdiction, it is important that proper venue also be established in the complaint. Venue refers to the geographic location of the federal court in which a claim may be properly brought. The federal court system is divided into judicial districts, which can cover the entire state or, in more populous states, a portion of the state. Venue rules ensure that suits are tried in a place which is related to the claims asserted or the parties to the action.

If the case is based on a federal question, 28 U.S.C. §1391 (b) provides for venue in (1) a judicial district where any defendant resides, if all defendants reside in the same state, (2) a judicial district in which a substantial part of the events giving rise to the claim occurred, or (3) a judicial district in which any defendant may be found, if there is no district in which the action may otherwise be brought. Generally, it is preferable to bring the claim in the district that has jurisdiction where the claim arose, or where the injury or events giving rise to the claim actually occurred.

In diversity lawsuits, 28 U.S.C. §1391 (a) states that proper venue may be in (1) a judicial district where any defendant resides, if all defendants reside in the same state, (2) a judicial district in which a substantial part of the events giving rise to the claim occurred, or (3) a judicial district in which any defendant is subject to personal jurisdiction at the time the actions is commenced, if there is no other district in which the action may otherwise be brought. If the defendants live in different states, you must file in the judicial district in which the claim arose.

I.   **THE PARTIES AND JURISDICTION**

        1.Plaintiff, SANFORD & SONS Limited, ("S&S"), is a limited company, organized under Swiss law, having its principal place of business in Berne, Switzerland.

        2.Defendant, CAC Aviation Corporation ("CAC") is a corporation, organized under New York law, having its principal place of business in Hamburg, New York.

FIGURE 30: Example identification of parties and jurisdiction

Statement of Claims/Causes of Action

Every complaint must assert at least one cause of action which is the legal principle that forms the basis of the claim. A premises liability cause of action, for instance, exists when an injury takes place on the property of another. Intentional tort claims are filed when the harm resulted from the intentional acts of another.

In order to successfully plead the case, the facts must support the elements of cause of action. Therefore, it is important to be familiar with both the facts of the case and law and legal principles involved. Set out each claim in numbered paragraphs, with each asserting a single occurrence or fact. Each paragraph builds on the other to establish the necessary elements of just one of the claims to be asserted against the other party.

> NOTE: Avoid legal conclusions or broad statements about cause of action. You wouldn't write "negligently hit the plaintiff's car" or "defendant is guilty of negligence". In a civil suit there is no guilt being determined, only liability. Instead write out the facts and actions that led to the suit for negligence. *See Figure 31.*

If the case involves multiple claims, each claim, or "count," should appear under its own heading ("Count I," "Count II," "Count III," etc.) Any allegations under that heading should relate specifically to that claim. To avoid repetition, allegations from prior paragraphs are incorporated by reference. For instance the second count may open with the following:

"Plaintiff repeats and re-alleges each and every allegation contained in paragraph one through paragraph seven hereof, with the same force and effect as if fully set forth herein."

The complaint may need to overcome a summary judgment motion or a motion for dismissal based on a failure to sufficiently state the cause of action. Some general matters to consider in preparing this section include the following;

- o Describe the facts in chronological order
- o Provide dates and times of each important event as precisely as possible
- o Identify and explain how each element of the claim has been met.
- o Briefly describe what each defendant did, or failed to do, and how those actions or failures to act caused injury
- o Describe any physical or emotional injury sustained, as well as any required treatment
- o Include names of other persons involved, dates and locations of described events
- o Do not to exaggerate the facts or make false statements
- o Avoid any conclusions of law
- o Do not inadvertently divulge trial strategies or allude to possible defenses
- o Use clear language and simple, direct statements
- o Describe each event in a separate numbered paragraph
- o Documents referenced should be labeled as exhibits and attached to the complaint

---

II. **FACTS**

3. On or about November 26, 2010, S&S and CAC entered into a CAC 500 Aircraft Deposit Agreement (the "Deposit Agreement") relating to the sale and delivery, on one hand, and the purchase, on the other hand, of a CAC S-730 model aircraft, for the Standard Aircraft Price amount of $1,520,000, exclusive of optional equipment, and as adjusted pursuant to an economic escalation formula.

4. As relevant to the matters contained in this complaint, the Deposit Agreement provides that S&S, as the buyer, would make an initial deposit of $25,000, followed by a series of pre-delivery payments and additional deposits, as follows: (1) $75,000 six (6) months after execution of the Deposit Agreement; and (2) $80,000 twelve (12) months after execution of the Deposit Agreement; and (3) up to sixty percent (60%) of the total amount six (6) months prior to scheduled delivery of the aircraft; and (4) unpaid balance, due at delivery.

FIGURE 31: Example statement of facts in a complaint

A Note on Pleading Standards

The standard for the structure, detail and substance of pleadings in the federal courts has changed throughout the course of American jurisprudence. Beginning in the late 1950's, the tendency, particularly in federal courts, was to simplify the standards to such an extent that a standardized form complaint may only have required the plaintiff summarize the relevant facts and specify the harm caused by the event. This is known as notice pleading.

Two relatively recent U.S. Supreme Court rulings, *Bell Atlantic Corp. v. Twombly*, 550 U.S. 544 (2007) and *Ashcroft v. Iqbal*, 556 U.S. 662 (2009), have heightened the pleading standards in federal courts. Fact-based pleading requires that the complaint include facts sufficient to demonstrate the plausibility of a party's claims and defenses at the earliest states of the case. In other words, the facts section of the complaint should sufficiently allege the elements of the claim.

III.   CLAIMS FOR RELIEF

Claim I.   Breach of Contract

13.   S&S hereby re-alleges and incorporates by reference the allegations in Paragraphs 1 – 12.

14.   CAC has failed to refund to S&S any of its pre-delivery payments and deposits pursuant to the terms of the Deposit Agreement, and thus breached that agreement.

15.   S&S has suffered damages as a result of CAC's breach of the Deposit Agreement.

WHEREFORE, S&S demands judgment against CAC in an amount to be proven at trial, and such other and further relief as may be just, proper and allowable, including its attorneys' fees, pre-judgment and post-judgment interest and the costs of this suit.

Claim II. Unjust Enrichment

16.   S&S hereby re-alleges and incorporates by reference the allegations in Paragraphs 1 – 15.

FIGURE 32: Example statement of the claim in a complaint

Prayer for relief

The prayer for relief reiterates the remedies sought for each count in the complaint. Relief refers to solutions or remedies that the court is able to provide and may include the following:

- o Declaratory relief
- o Injunctive relief
- o Compensatory Damages
- o Punitive Damages (where appropriate)
- o Fees and/or costs (as appropriate)
- o In addition, the prayer generally concludes with a request for "Such other and further relief" at the discretion of the court.

Each type of relief must be supported by the factual allegations and legal claims that precede it. If the court's jurisdiction depends on a minimum or maximum amount of monetary damages, your demand must meet that requirement. For example, damages must exceed $75,000 in diversity cases.

The prayer is typically a single paragraph with sub-paragraphs where appropriate. Unlike other paragraphs, it is not numbered, but rather, begins with the phrasing "Wherefore, the defendant prays…." Hence, it is frequently referred to as the "Wherefore clause." *See Figure 33 for an example.*

Signature

The signature block follows the prayer for relief and attests to the truth and veracity of the contents of the complaint. As always, check local court rules for specific requirements, but under FRCP 11(a), all complaints must be signed by at least one attorney of record in the attorney's name (or by an unrepresented plaintiff) and, at a minimum, contain the address, email address and telephone number of the signer.

FRCP 11(b)(1-4) stipulates that, in signing, the attorney or pro se plaintiff certifies to the best of his or her knowledge, information and belief, formed after an inquiry reasonable under the circumstances, that:

- o The complaint is not being presented for any improper purpose, such as to harass, cause unnecessary delay or needlessly increase the cost of litigation
- o The claims are warranted by existing law or by a non-frivolous argument for extending, modifying or reversing existing law or for establishing new law
- o The factual contentions have evidentiary support or, if specifically identified, will likely have evidentiary support after a reasonable opportunity for discovery

○ The denials of factual contentions are warranted on the evidence or, if specifically identified, are reasonably based on belief or a lack of information

WHEREFORE, Sanford & Sons, LTD demands judgment against CAC Corporation in an amount to be proven at trial, and such other and further relief as may be just, proper and allowable, including pre-judgment and post-judgment interest and the costs of this suit.

Dated this 5th Day of December, 2012

Respectfully submitted,

HACKNEY & IMP, LLP

/s/ Mumfort J. Sharken
Lawrence Kimbell
Mumfort J. Sharken Post
Office Box 6842
Hamburg, New York 06000-6842 (555)
555-4734
(555) 555-6043 (facsimile)

FIGURE 33: Example prayer for relief and signature

Demand for jury trial, if desired

In federal court cases, the right to a jury trial is governed by federal law. Generally, actions seeking monetary damages are eligible for trial by jury when requested, whereas actions seeking specific performance, injunctions and other non-monetary damages must be heard by a judge.

The court may strike a jury demand if it determines that no federal right exists

○ Under FRCP 38 a party may demand a trial by jury through a written demand which may be included within a pleading no later than 14 days after the last pleading is served.

○ A party waives its right to a jury trial unless the jury demand is properly served and filed (FRCP 38(d)). If a party does not properly demand a jury, the issues are tried by a judge.

- o Normally, the jury trial is requested by entering "Demand for Jury Trial" in the caption of the complaint. In some jurisdictions, the demand is also included in the prayer for relief; be sure to check your local rules of court.

- o FRCP 38(c) allows a party to request a jury trial on select issues only, if desired. If the opposing party wishes to have additional issues tried by a jury, they may make the demand within 14 days.

- o If the plaintiff has previously filed the jury demand, the defendant may rely on that demand and, therefore, does not need to make a separate demand for the same issues.

- o If the plaintiff wishes to withdraw a demand for jury trial, they must obtain consent of the defendant to ensure that the defendant may then file their own demand, if desired.

Summons for federal court case

The summons notifies the defendant that they are being sued. A summons must be prepared for each defendant and submitted to the court clerk along with a copy of the complaint. If the summons is in proper form, the clerk will sign it, affix the court and return it to the plaintiff, at which time, process may be served.

The Summons should be obtained immediately upon filing the complaint so that service is rendered promptly. The action is subject to dismissal if summons is not served within 120 days after filing of the complaint

A proper summons must:

- o Name the court and the parties
- o Be directed to the defendant
- o State the name and address of the plaintiff's attorney
- o State when the defendant must appear and defend
- o Notify the defendant that a failure to appear and defend will result in a default judgment against the defendant for the relief demanded in the complaint
- o Be signed by the clerk
- o Bear the court's seal

See Figure 34 for an example summons.

UNITED STATES DISTRICT COURT

for the

District of Colorado

MARY ANN GILLIGAN	)
_____	)
Plaintiff(s)	)
v.	) Civil Action No. CV-00000-00-2011
	)
	)
	)
GINGER K. HOWELL	)
_____	)
Defendant(s)	)

SUMMONS IN A CIVIL ACTION

To: GINGER K. HOWELL
575 BOULDER BLVD. APT. #4
CLINTON, COLORADO 00007

A lawsuit has been filed against you.

Within 21 days after service of this summons on you (not counting the day you received it) — or 60 days if you are the United States or a United States agency, or an officer or employee of the United States described in Fed. R. Civ. 12 (a)(2) or (3) — you must serve on the plaintiff an answer to the attached complaint or a motion under Rule 12 of the Federal Rules of Civil Procedure. The answer or motion must be served on the plaintiff or plaintiff's attorney, whose name and address are:

COLLINS FORTHWRIGHT III, ESQ.
1696 LINCOLN PLACE
SUITE 7207
GORE, COLORADO 00070

If you fail to respond, judgment by default will be entered against you for the relief demanded in the complaint. You also must file your answer or motion with the court.

CLERK OF COURT

Date: _____5/14/2011_____   *Lovey Jameson*
                                        _____
                                        Signature of Clerk or Deputy Clerk

FIGURE 34: Example Federal Summons

SERVICE OF PROCESS

Service of process is simply the delivery of the summons and complaint to the defendants. The rules governing service of process set forth strict requirements which must be followed closely, as improper service may invalidate any future proceedings. Proper service provides the defendant with reasonable notice and grants the court jurisdiction over the defendant.

Most district courts are implementing electronic filing which will require that pleadings be filed using the internet. The rules regarding electronic filing differ greatly from jurisdiction to jurisdiction. You should check your local rules of court regarding the methods of handling electronic filing and follow them closely.

In federal proceedings, the plaintiff must serve each defendant with copies of the summons and complaint. If a case has multiple defendants and the plaintiff prepared one summons listing all names, a signed and sealed summons must be issued for and served upon each defendant.

Generally, the plaintiff must serve a defendant located in a judicial district of the U.S. with the summons and complaint within 120 days after the complaint is filed. If the plaintiff does not serve the defendant within 120 days of filing the complaint, the court, after notifying the plaintiff, must on its own or on motion either:

- o Dismiss the action without prejudice
- o Order that service be made within a specified time

Depending on the circumstances, the summons, complaint and other case initiating documents must be served by either:

- o A non-party adult chosen by plaintiff's counsel. Generally, any person who is at least 18 years old and not a party to the action may serve the case initiating documents on the defendant. For example, an attorney might utilize a staff member or hire an outside process server
- o A U.S. marshal, deputy marshal or another person appointed by the court

Generally, the plaintiff may serve an individual located in a judicial district of the U.S. through any of the following methods:

- o Personally delivering a copy of the summons and complaint to the individual.
- o Leaving a copy of the summons and complaint at the individual's residence with another resident of suitable age and judgment.
- o Personally delivering a copy of the summons and complaint to an agent authorized by appointment or by law to receive service of process.

- ○ Following state law for service in an action brought in a court of general jurisdiction in the state where:
  - the district court is located; or
  - service is made

In an effort to encourage cooperation between parties, and to eliminate the costs of effecting service, FRCP 4(d) provides for "waiver of service" which:

- ○ authorizes plaintiffs to send defendants a notice of the action and a request for waiver of service
- ○ imposes upon defendants a duty to avoid the costs of service
- ○ encourages defendants to waive service by offering the incentive of additional time to respond. A defendant located in a judicial district of the U.S. who waives service has 60 days to respond to the complaint.
- ○ imposes a "penalty" of shifting the costs of service if defendants fail to waive

The defendant should be notified that the action has been commenced, and a request for waiver should be provided. The notice and request should:

- ○ Be in writing and addressed to:
  - the individual defendant; or
  - for a corporation, partnership or association, to an officer, general or managing agent or other agent authorized by appointment or by law to receive service of process
- ○ State the name of the court where the complaint was filed
- ○ Be accompanied by:
  - a copy of the complaint;
  - two copies of the waiver form; and
  - a pre-paid return envelope
- ○ Inform the defendant of the consequences of waiving and not waiving service
- ○ State the date the request was sent
- ○ Give the defendant a reasonable period of time of at least 30 days after the request was sent (or at least 60 days if sent to the defendant outside the U.S.) to return the waiver
- ○ Be sent by first-class mail or other reliable means, such as electronically or by private messenger service

A request to waive formal service of process should be sent to the defendant immediately after commencing the action, as the plaintiff must file the waiver form signed by the defendant within 120 days after the complaint is filed. If the defendant fails to respond to the request, the plaintiff is required to effect service. Relevant specifications under FRCP apply as if a summons and complaint were served on the date the plaintiff files the signed waiver.

If the plaintiff files a waiver of service signed by the defendant, the plaintiff does not need to file proof of service. Instead, the defendant signs and returns the waiver within 60 days. The signed waiver serves as acknowledgment because it is received along with 5.

Notice

Due process requires that the defendant have adequate notice and a case may be dismissed if the defendant did not receive proper notice of the action against him. Under FRCP 4, service of process is used to ensure that the defendant has adequate notice that a legal action has been filed against him.

Typically, the person who serves the defendant is required to show proof of service, usually in the form of an affidavit of service which must be filed with the court. In most federal district courts, the summons typically includes a return of service containing a declaration to be signed by the process server.

Acknowledgement

The affidavit of service made by a person who serves the summons and complaint serves as both proof and acknowledgment of service. In essence, the person rendering process serves as a witness, so the defendant's personal acknowledgment is unnecessary. In other circumstances, an acknowledgment of receipt is necessary to avoid any possible future denials and consequent motions to dismiss.

If the parties agree that the defendant or the defendant's attorney will simply accept the summons and complaint most courts use a *Receipt and Acknowledgment of Acceptance of Service* or similar form which the defendant signs, dates, and returns.

When the defendant agrees to waive service under FRCP 4(d) the summons and complaint are served by mail. The defendant signs and returns the waiver within 60 days, thus acknowledging receipt. Since the plaintiff files a waiver of service signed by the defendant, the plaintiff does not need to file proof of service. *See Figure 35 for an example notice and acknowledgment.*

UNITED STATES DISTRICT COURT	DISTRICT OF COLORADO

MARY ANN GILLIGAN	§	
Plaintiff(s),	§	
	§	
versus	§	CIVIL ACTION NO. CV-00000-00-2011
GINGER K. HOWELL	§	
Defendant(s).	§	

NOTICE AND ACKNOWLEDGMENT FOR SERVICE BY MAIL

TO DEFENDANT: GINGER K. HOWELL 575 Boulder Blvd. #4 Clinton, Colorado 00007
(Name and Address)

The summons and complaint are served under Rule 4(c)(2)(C)(ii) of the Federal Rules of Civil Procedure. You must sign and date the acknowledgment below and return one copy of it to the sender within 20 days. If you received the papers for a corporation, unincorporated association, partnership, or other entity (including another person), you must indicate under your signature and your relationship to it.

If you *do not* return the completed form to the sender within 20 days, you may be required to pay the expenses of serving a summons and complaint in another way under the law.

If you *do* return the completed form, you must answer the complaint within 20 days. If you fail to file an answer, a judgment will be taken against you for the relief demanded in the complaint.

I declare, under the penalty of perjury, that this notice and acknowledgment will have been mailed on ____5/14/2011_____.

Mary Ann Gilligan
_____
Signature of Plaintiff
5/14/2011
_____
Date of Signature

ACKNOWLEDGMENT OF RECEIPT

I declare, under penalty of perjury, that I received a copy of the summons and complaint in this matter on ____5/17/2011_____ at ____575 Boulder Blvd. #4 Clinton, Colorado 00007___.
(date)   (location)

Ginger K. Howell
_____
Signature
Ginger K. Howell
_____
Name Typed
Self
_____
Relationship or Authority

FIGURE 35: Example Notice and Acknowledgment of Service

RESPONSIVE PLEADINGS

Upon learning of the claim, the defendant must respond to the allegations set forth in the complaint. Failure to respond will result in default, and possible judgment against the defendant. Depending on the circumstances and/or advice of counsel, the response may take the form an answer, or a motion to dismiss.

The answer is the defendant's formal, written response to the plaintiff's allegations in the complaint, wherein the defendant admits or denies the plaintiff's contentions and states any defenses. A motion to dismiss is a formal written request filed with the court, requesting that the case be dismissed. Pursuant to FRCP 12, the time in which responsive pleadings must be filed in federal court is as follows:

- 21 days following standard service of process
- 60 days following timely waiver of domestic service
- 90 days following timely waiver of foreign service

The Answer

The answer to the Complaint is generally double-spaced with the first line of each paragraph indented 5 to 10 spaces. The answer includes the following:

- Case caption, which must appear exactly as it does on the Complaint

- Preamble – not numbered

- Body – numbered consecutively responding to and specifying the paragraphs containing each allegation set forth in the Complaint

- Signature Line

- Certificate of Service/Mailing

As noted previously, in matters involving multiple plaintiffs or defendants it is appropriate to name just the first party, followed by "et al," in all documents subsequent to the complaint. That is, however, the only permissible change to the caption. If minor errors are noted, they should be addressed in the body of the complaint. More significant errors will require amending the caption through a motion or stipulation.

The document title should identify should identify the answering party as well as the pleading to which the party is replying (e.g., DEFENDANT'S ANSWER TO THE PLAINTIFF'S COMPLAINT).

The body of the answer addresses each paragraph as set forth in the complaint, and may open with a brief introduction identifying the attorney, the answering defendant and the pleading to which the answer replies. Subsequent sections should include appropriate headings (i.e., General Allegations, Defenses, Crossclaims, etc.) were applicable.

The defendant must then either admit or deny the allegations within each paragraph of the complaint in sequence FRCP 8(b). Once an allegation is admitted, it is accepted as true for the entire case. Any allegation that is not denied will be deemed admitted by the court. Therefore, care must be taken to respond to each allegation in full.

A defendant may deny any allegation it believes to be false, but must plead with specificity certain denials pursuant to FRCP 9. For example, if the defendant wants to deny a party's legal existence or capacity to sue or be sued, it must plead the denial with specificity, stating any facts that are peculiarly within its knowledge (FRCP 9(a)).

A denial must fairly respond to the substance of the allegation. A party that intends in good faith to deny only part of an allegation must admit the part that is true and deny the rest. (e.g., "Defendant admits that she entered into a contract with Plaintiff on the date specified, but denies all other allegations in Paragraph 7 of the complaint").

If an informed conclusion cannot be reached regarding the truth of an allegation, the defendant may plead a "lack of knowledge or information sufficient to form a belief about the truth of the allegation, in which case, the response is treated as a denial".

The prayer for relief generally asks that the plaintiff be denied relief, and the defendant be awarded costs and other relief to as deemed just and proper.

Unlike a complaint, the answer requires a Certificate of Service which is a statement of the date and manner in which a copy of the document was served on a party or counsel of record. The certificate should include information regarding the method of service, the date of service, and the names and addresses of those served. A certificate of service should be prepared for all responsive pleadings, motions and discovery requests.

As a final note, if the defendant was served with a verified complaint (generally not required in federal court) the answer must also be verified. A verified complaint is one in which the plaintiff swears under oath that, to the best of their knowledge, the allegations set forth in the complaint are true. *See Figure 36 in this chapter and also Appendix B for an example answer.*

Caption omitted

DEFENDANT'S ANSWER TO COMPLAINT FOR BREACH OF CONTRACT, UNJUST ENRICHMENT, AND CONVERSION

Defendant CAC Aviation Corporation, a New York corporation ("CAC"), by counsel, for its answer to the plaintiff's Complaint for Breach of Contract, Unjust Enrichment, and Conversion, filed on December 5, 2012 (the "Complaint"), states:

FIRST DEFENSE

1. CAC is without knowledge sufficient to admit or deny the allegations in paragraph 1 of the Complaint, and therefore denies the allegations.

2. CAC admits the allegations in paragraph 2 of the Complaint.

3. CAC admits the allegations in paragraph 3 of the Complaint.

4. CAC is without knowledge sufficient to admit or deny the allegations in paragraph 4 of the Complaint, and therefore denies the allegations.

5. In response to the allegations in paragraph 5 of the Complaint, CAC states that agreement referred to speaks for itself, and denies the allegations to the extent inconsistent with the agreement.

FIGURE 36: Example elements of an answer

Affirmative Defenses

Affirmative defenses are facts or circumstances that defeat the plaintiff's claim even if the factual allegations of the other party's claims are admitted or proven. To assert an affirmative defense, the defendant must plead or describe the facts that constitute the defense. The general rule under FRCP 8(c) is that affirmative defenses must be raised in the answer or will be waived. Some of the affirmative defenses listed under 8(c) include but are not limited to:

- o Accord and satisfaction
- o Arbitration and award
- o Assumption of risk
- o Contributory negligence
- o Duress

- o Fraud
- o Illegality
- o Statute of frauds
- o Statute of limitations
- o Waiver

It should be noted that each court may apply rules regarding the pleading of defenses. Therefore, this is another area in which it may be necessary to consult case law, as well as the rules of court prior to proceeding.

Under Rule 10(b), the affirmative defenses should be listed sequentially as "Defendant's First Affirmative Defense," "Defendant's Second Affirmative Defense," etc., in numbered paragraphs continuing the paragraph numbering in the allegations. Facts need not be alleged to support affirmative defenses unless required to plead with particularity pursuant to Rule 9.

MOTIONS

A motion is a written request wherein the moving party, or movant, asks the court to grant an order or take some other action. The granting of a dispositive motion, such as a motion to dismiss, or a motion for summary judgment, can resolve an entire legal claim, and the number of civil cases resolved through dispositive motions far exceeds those that go to trial. Motions, therefore, can be critical in civil litigation.

The exact form of a motion varies, but at its core a motion contains two fundamental elements: the request for relief and the argument. The relief generally involves a request that the court take action, such as issuing an order, dismissing a claim or part of a claim, or extending a deadline. The argument analyzes relevant legal authority and persuasively states its relevance to the client's position based on existing facts. Typically, the arguments are made to the court in a legal memorandum. Facts in support of a motion may be established by appending an affidavit, which in turn, may authenticate and/or explain attached documents.

FRCP 7(b)(1) requires that all motions, other than those made at trial, be made in writing and state with particularity the grounds supporting the motion and the relief or order sought. The specifics of motion practice, however, are governed by local rules of court and rules known as standing orders, which are issued by the judge. These rules exist to clarify, among other things, the time limits for bringing a motion, the required or permitted supporting documents, and the right to present oral arguments.

A motion hearing allows the attorneys to present factual evidence and legal arguments relevant to the motion. While a judge may call for a motion hearing at their discretion, it is commonly requested by counsel for one of the parties. In some jurisdictions, the request is included in the motion's caption, and in others it is a separate document. A request for oral argument is typically made in writing at the time the motion is filed, though some courts require that a hearing date be secured prior to filing and service of the motion.

Motions must be filed with the court and served upon all parties. If a motion hearing is required, the party bringing the motion may schedule a hearing with the court clerk and notice must be provided to the opposing party. Under the rules governing the claim, the party is allowed a specific period of time during which all parties must be served with the motion and all other papers. Under the federal rules, the moving party must serve and file the following.

Notice of Motion

Upon or before a motion is filed with the court, the movant must serve the opposing party with a notice of motion. The notice of motion informs the opposing party that the motion has been filed and indicates when the court will hear the motion, thus providing ample opportunity to prepare for the hearing. Pursuant to FRCP 6(c) a written notice of motion must typically be served at least 14 days prior to the hearing. In some circumstances, service upon the attorney of record may be sufficient but, typically under the federal rules, the notice of motion must be served upon all parties.

Notice may be provided as a separate document or within the motion itself. If notice is included within the motion, the title of the document should reflect this. (i.e., *Notice of Motion and Motion to Dismiss*) The notice should state the relief sought, when and in what court the motion will be made, the papers, if any, upon which it will be based, and the time in which to respond. If a hearing date has been secured, it is typically stated in the notice though, in some jurisdictions, a notice of hearing will be provided by the court.

Motion

The judicial system encompasses a vast number of courts, each imposing its own pre-trial procedures. As a result, it is not unusual to encounter inconsistencies regarding the form in which motions are filed with the court.

IN THE UNITED STATES DISTRICT COURT
FOR THE
DISTRICT OF COLORADO

Honorable Judgely C. DoRight

JANE DOE,

        Plaintiff,

                         Case No. 999-AA-9999 (XXX)

v.

MABLE ABLE

        Defendant,

NOTICE OF MOTION TO DISMISS FOR FAILURE TO STATE A CLAIM

UPON WHICH RELIEF CAN BE GRANTED

To: Jane Doe, and Lawrence T. Lawrence, her attorney

Please take notice that:

On May 18, 2011, at 2 o'clock p.m., or as soon as counsel may be heard, in the courtroom of the above-entitled court at the courthouse at 123 Baker Street, City of Happy, County of Sadd, in the State of Colorado, Defendant, Mable Able will move the court to dismiss plaintiff's complaint for failure to state a claim upon which relief can be granted.

                                               Respectfully submitted,

Dated: March 25, 2011

                                        Martin J. Mushbottom
                                       Martin J. Mushbottom
                                    Attorney for the Defendant
                                    657 Orchard St.
                                    Stanford, CT 01010
                                    (555) 555-8934

FIGURE 37: Example Notice of Motion to Dismiss

IN THE UNITED STATES DISTRICT COURT
FOR THE
DISTRICT OF COLORADO

Honorable Judgely C. DoRight

JANE DOE,

        Plaintiff,

                                     Case No. 999-AA-9999 (XXX)

v.

MABLE ABLE

        Defendant.

MOTION TO DISMISS FOR FAILURE TO STATE A CLAIM

UPON WHICH RELIEF CAN BE GRANTED

To: Jane Doe, and Lawrence T. Lawrence, her attorney

COME NOW, Defendant Mable Able, by Martin J. Mushbottom, her attorney, moves the court to dismiss the Plaintiff's Complaint on the following grounds that the Plaintiff has failed to state a claim upon which relief can be granted.

Dated: March 25, 2011

Respectfully submitted,

Martin J. Mushbottom
Martin J. Mushbottom
Attorney for the Defendant
657 Orchard St.
Stanford, CT 01010
(555) 555-8934
mjmushbottom@lawfirm.com

FIGURE 38: Example Motion to Dismiss

The motion is formatted much like pleadings, and includes:

- o   the name of the court
- o   the case caption
- o   the title of the motion
- o   the body or text
- o   the relief requested
- o   the attorney's signature

The title should state the specific type of motion (i.e., MOTION FOR MORE DEFINITE STATEMENT). The body of the motion should include the nature of the motion, the party submitting the papers and, where applicable, details regarding the hearing including the date, time and judge's name. Where warranted, paragraphs should be numbered.

In the federal courts, a motion must state with particularity the grounds upon which the motion is made and must set forth the relief or order sought (FRCP 7(b)(1)). This may or may not apply in a state court and, once again, local rules must be consulted.

Affidavits, exhibits and other supporting documents should be described, tabbed in sequence and served with the other papers. Under FRCP 5(d) papers to be served on opposing parties must be presented for filing "together with a certificate of service." In all jurisdictions, the motion must be signed by the attorney of record.

Motions are filed with the court and a copy is furnished to the opposing party. If a motion hearing is required, the party bringing the motion may schedule a hearing with the court clerk and a notice should be provided to the opposing party. Pursuant to your state rules, motions must be served upon all parties within a specified period of time prior to hearing and should include all supporting affidavits and legal memos.

Notice of Hearing

The moving party must file the motion and notify the court to request a hearing. The decision as to whether or not to hold a hearing on a motion is generally at the discretion of the court unless otherwise specified by rule or statute. Written notice of the hearing of all motions must be provided to all parties to ensure that they have adequate time to prepare. The scheduling of motion hearings differs from court to court. Some courts specify hearing days and in others, the hearing is scheduled through the court clerk.

In federal court, the notice of hearing must identify the judge, the case name and docket number, the title of the motion and the date and time of the hearing. The court clerk schedules the hearing which the movant must then enter on the notice. The notice must be mailed within the time specified by rule or statute.

Caption Omitted

NOTICE OF HEARING

To: Jane Doe, and Lawrence T. Lawrence, her attorney

Please take notice that:

The motion to dismiss in the above-captioned matter is set for argument in the courtroom of Judge DoRight on May 18, 2011, at 2 o'clock p.m., or as soon as the clerk calls the matter.

Respectfully submitted,

Dated: March 25, 2011

Martin J. Mushbottom
Martin J. Mushbottom
Attorney for the Defendant
657 Orchard St.
Stanford, CT 01010
(555) 555-8934

FIGURE 39: Example Notice of Hearing

Affidavit

An affidavit is a voluntary, written statement of fact made under oath or affirmation. The fundamental nature of some motions, such as those presenting defenses under FRCP 12(b)(2) through (5), for example, requires factual showings based on personal knowledge. Affidavits are introduced to verify the facts upon which the motion is based, or to authenticate evidentiary exhibits, and may be obtained from any person competent to testify including parties, witnesses, experts, and in some instances, attorneys.

Affidavits should be properly captioned for the legal matter, and the title should reflect the name of the witness, or *affiant,* as well as the motion to which it applies. (i.e., AFFIDAVIT OF JOHN BROWN IN SUPPORT OF DEFENDANT'S MOTION FOR SUMMARY JUDGMENT).

An introductory clause, or preamble, immediately follows the title and states the full name of the affiant and affirms that the statement is offered under oath. (i.e., "John C. Brown, being duly sworn, deposes and says…") The remaining body of the affidavit consists of the specific factual claims presented through sequentially numbered paragraphs.

FRCP 56(c)(4) specifies that the affidavit must allege the affiant's competency to testify on the matters stated, and should "set out facts that would be admissible in evidence." The affiant must have personal knowledge of the facts stated therein, and the statement itself must offer facts from which that person's knowledge can naturally be inferred.

In some instances, it may be possible to introduce statements not based on genuine personal knowledge, such as those based on opinion, or necessarily dependent on information derived from others, upon the affiants "information and belief." The permissibility of such statements, however, may be limited by circumstances, the nature of the motion and, in some jurisdictions, expressly prohibited by statute. Hence, thorough research should be conducted prior to relying on an affidavit in which allegations are offered solely on information and belief.

Finally, because the affidavit functions as sworn testimony, the affiant must appear before a notary and swear to its truth and veracity. At that time, the affidavit will be signed, the notary statement, or *jurat,* will be executed, and the affidavit will be ready for filing and service.

Motion to Dismiss

A motion to dismiss the complaint argues that there are technical issues in the way it was written, filed, or served. A motion to dismiss should be filed before filing an answer or any other responsive pleading and, unless otherwise specified, is due when the defendant's answer would have been due. A timely filed motion to dismiss extends defendant's time to file a responsive pleading. If the court denies the motion, the defendant's responsive pleading is due 14 days after notice of the court's action, even if the defendant is only moving to dismiss some of plaintiff's claims.

COUNTY OF ORANGE   :   STATE OF CALIFORNIA
AMHERST TOWN COURT :   HONORABLE JUDGE JUDGE

LARRY LANDOWNER

                    Plaintiff,

vs.   **AFFIDAVIT IN SUPPORT**
                                                       OF MOTION

PETER PURCHASER,

                    Defendant,

STATE OF CALIFORNIA   )
COUNTY OF ORANGE   ) ss:
)

I, LAWRENCE TRUEBLOOD, being duly sworn and deposes and says:

1)   I am one of the attorneys of record for the defendant in this cause and am fully

      familiar with the facts and circumstances surrounding this case.

2)   The original deed from Larry Landowner to Peter Purchaser, dated April 3, 2013, and

      filed for record with Orange County Clerk-Recorder on April 5, 2013, and recorded

      in Book 2741, page 1568 of the Orange County Records, conveying land in

      controversy in this suit has been lost.

3)   The defendant and his attorney cannot procure the original deed.

                                                       Respectfully submitted,

                                                       Lawrence Trueblood
                                                       Lawrence Trueblood
                                                       Defendant's Attorney
                                                       6176 Orange St.
                                                       Orange, CA 00010
                                                       (555) 555-8841
                                                       ltrueblood@lawfirm.com

Subscribed and sworn to before me this _____ *day of* _____ *, 20* ____ .

_____ *Notary Public*

FIGURE 40: Example Affidavit

Under FRCP 12(b) the following seven defenses may be made by motion if the defendant desires:

- o FRCP 12(b) (1) lack of jurisdiction over the subject matter of the case
- o FRCP 12(b) (2) lack of jurisdiction over the person
- o FRCP 12(b) (3) improper venue
- o FRCP 12(b) (4) insufficiency of process
- o FRCP 12(b) (5) insufficiency of service of process
- o FRCP 12(b) (6) failure to state a claim upon which relief can be granted
- o FRCP 12(b) (7) failure to join an indispensable party under Rule 19

Making a motion to dismiss is a strategic decision. Depending on the circumstances, a well-founded motion to dismiss can dispose of a case entirely, limit the issues in a case, avoid unnecessary costs of discovery and trial or force the plaintiff to show support for his claims.

Generally, a motion to dismiss under FRCP 12(b)(1)-(7) will be decided before trial unless the court orders a deferral until trial. In ruling on the motion, the court may grant the motion, in whole or in part; deny the motion; or grant the motion with leave to amend, if there are errors that may be fixed by the plaintiff. If leave to amend is granted, the plaintiff must submit an amended complaint within the time specified at which time the defendant must either file the answer, or another motion. *See Figure 38 for an example motion to dismiss.*

Motion for a More Definite Statement

While not a defense, the motion for more definite statement is frequently filed prior to any responsive pleading. Sometimes, a complaint is so vague, ambiguous or lacking in detail that the defendant cannot reasonably respond. In these instances, FRCP 12(e) allows the defendant to move the court to order a more definite statement from the plaintiff. This motion can only be filed when a party is unable to respond to the allegations, and is not an attempt to challenge the plaintiff's claim. For instance, the defendant cannot simply request further details, or seek to have an allegation included or withdrawn.

A motion for a more definite statement may only be filed in response to a pleading which requires or allows a responsive pleading, such as those set forth under FRCP 7(a). For example, a party cannot seek a more definite statement in response to a motion to dismiss, or a special defense. The motion itself must specifically identify what the party requires in order to adequately respond, and cannot be made after the defendant has already filed any responsive pleading.

If the motion is granted, the plaintiff must obey the order within 14 days after notice of the order unless the court sets a different deadline (FRCP 12(a)(4)(B)). If the plaintiff does not revise the complaint according to the order, the court may strike the complaint, or issue other appropriate orders. Typically, the plaintiff will file an amended complaint, at which time the defendant has 14 days to file a responsive pleading as specified in FRCP 12 (a)(4)(b).

Ex Parte Motion

An *ex parte* motion is a motion requesting that the court act without the other party being notified. *Ex parte* motions request temporary emergency relief, such as an emergency request for continuance or a temporary restraining order.

Understandably, the courts can be reluctant to act on *ex parte* motions, as the opposing party is not provided with an opportunity to challenge the claims of the movant. Therefore, the moving party must typically show first, that time is of the essence if their cause is to avoid being "irreparably prejudiced," and second, that the crisis is not due to the movant's own negligence.

It is imperative that local rules of court be consulted prior to filing any *ex parte* motion, as each jurisdiction has its own requirements. Under the federal rules, an application for *ex parte* relief should be in writing, and include the following:

- Application containing the case caption, and stating the relief requested

- Memorandum of points and authorities setting forth the legal basis for the relief requested

- Affidavit setting forth whatever facts are necessary for *ex parte* relief

- Affidavit showing "good cause" for *ex parte* relief. Examples of "good cause" include:

    - Existence of a genuine emergency, threatening immediate and irreparable injury

    - Danger that properly noticing the opposition poses the risk that the party might flee, destroy evidence or hide assets

    - Routine nature of the relief requested does not require that the other party be given notice. For instance, seeking permission to exceed the length of a legal memorandum

    - Proposed order.

Dispositive Judgment

A dispositive motion asks the court to dispose of one or more claims in favor of the moving party without the need for further trial court proceedings. The motion to dismiss is filed in response to deficiencies in the complaint or service of process and was discussed earlier in the chapter. A motion for summary judgment is filed when no material facts appear to be in dispute, and hence, a ruling can be determined without the need for trial. If a party fails to respond to a pleading, the opposing party may file a motion to obtain default judgment.

Default judgment

The motion for default judgment requests that the court rule in favor of the plaintiff on all claims due to the defendant's failure to respond. Default judgments are based on the theory that in failing to respond, the party "admits the cause of action is valid, admits [it] has no defense, and consents to suffer judgment." If granted, the court will file judgment against the defendant. If the party wishes to dispute a default judgment, a motion to set aside the default judgment is required.

FRCP 55 provides for both the entry of default and the entry of a default judgment. An entry of default results from the failure to respond, but is not the default judgment itself.

Request to Enter Default

If a party fails to respond to a pleading within the time designated, they are considered to be "in default" at which time they become vulnerable to a default judgment. However, it is important to note that judgment has not, at that point, been rendered against the offending party. The entry of default is a preliminary order, entered in anticipation of a final judgment for default. Obtaining the default judgment requires several additional steps.

Upon detecting the failure to respond, the claimant files an affidavit stating that the defending party has failed to plead or defend, and requesting an entry of default. Under the federal rules, it is not necessary to notify the offending party that the application for default has been entered. If the party appears before the motion to enter default is filed they may respond. Once the motion is filed, however, they may not respond to the pleading without obtaining permission from the court.

Once the default has been verified, the clerk is authorized under FRCP 55(a) to enter the default in the file or on the docket sheet. Procedurally, until the default has been entered, the motion for default judgment is not permitted.

Once the default is entered, the offending party is no longer entitled to further notice regarding the litigation unless they appear. FRCP 55(c) allows the court to vacate the default if the defendant acts promptly and has an adequate excuse.

Affidavit

The form, purpose and substance of affidavits are discussed earlier in this chapter. Again, it is important to note that obtaining the default judgment will required the filing of two affidavits with the court. The first is filed with the application for entry of default. The second supports the motion for judgment on the default.

Entry of default judgment

FRCP 55 allows for two methods of entry judgments by default. Under 55(b)(1) the judgment may be entered by the court clerk under the following conditions:

- o The party in default must be competent

- o The claim must be for a specific sum, or one that can be definitively calculated

- o The party must not have appeared in the action. For purposes of default, an appearance is any action demonstrating sufficient interest, including participation in settlement negotiations, correspondence or other actions which is not consistent with abandonment of the proceedings.

If, and only if, each of these elements is met, the clerk is authorized to enter judgment for the amount due plus costs. In all other circumstances, the claimant must motion the court for judgment and request a hearing under FRCP 55(b)(2).

The court may set aside the default judgment under 60(b) on the grounds of mistake, inadvertence, excusable neglect, newly discovered evidence, fraud, satisfaction, or other reasons justifying such a decision.

Motion for Summary Judgment

Summary judgment may be warranted on a claim if the pleadings, discovery, affidavits, etc., show that the case involves no issue of fact that can be tried. Instead, the motion asserts that the claim only involves issues of law which can be decided based on the information available. Under Rule 56, a party may move for summary judgment upon all or any part of the claim.

The motion for summary judgment requires a great deal of preparation because the initial burden lies upon the movant to clearly establish the lack of factual issues. As a result, all pre-trial evidence must be reviewed and analyzed to successfully demonstrate grounds for judgment. In addition, many local rules impose format and content specifications that are not required in other motions.

In addition to the motion itself, the memorandum of points and authorities is required and must set forth the following:

- The claims for which summary judgment is sought
- The summary judgment standard based on the court's jurisdiction and legal authority applying the standard
- The legal elements for the claims on which summary judgment is sought, based on the court's jurisdiction
- Arguments regarding the absence of genuine issues of material fact to support the aforementioned elements
  - Supported by reference to pleadings, discovery affidavits, and other exhibits and supporting documents which should be tabbed in sequence and served with the other papers
- Legal arguments as to why judgment as a matter of law on the particular claim is appropriate

Some jurisdictions require a Statement of Material Facts Not in Dispute as a separate document. In addition, an appendix including all evidence, in sequence, to be considered in ruling on the motion may be specified by court order, local rules or party stipulation.

Unless a different time is set under local rules or the court orders otherwise, a party may file a motion for summary judgment at any time until 30 days after the close of discovery. A party against whom summary judgment is sought must be served with a notice of motion as specified by statute or court rule unless the party waives notice. Under the FRCP 6(e), the motion for summary judgment must be served at least 10 days before the time fixed for hearing.

Motion for judgment on the pleadings

Under FRCP 12(c) a motion for judgment on the pleadings is the proper procedure when all material allegations of fact are admitted in the pleadings and only questions of law remain. An example would be a complaint failing to allege the elements of a claim. It provides for judgment on the merits disposing of baseless claims and defenses, with the ultimate goals of avoiding the time and expense of discovery and trial.

The motion applies to pleadings and related replies named in FRCP 7(a), and may be filed any time after pleadings are closed, but sufficiently preceding trial to avoid delay. Pleadings are considered closed when the final reply to any and all pleadings has been filed. Any party may move the court for judgment on the pleadings.

IN THE UNITED STATES DISTRICT COURT
FOR THE
DISTRICT OF COLORADO

Honorable Judgely C. DoRight

JANE DOE,

        Plaintiff,

Case No. 999-AA-9999 (XXX)

v.

MABLE ABLE

        Defendant.

MOTION FOR SUMMARY JUDGMENT

Sam DeMann, defendant in the above-entitled action, moves the court that it enter, pursuant to Fed. R. Civ. P. 56(b), summary judgment in favor of defendant. This motion is made on the ground that under Fed. R. Civ. P. 41(a)(1), two voluntary dismissals of actions based on or including the claim asserted in this action operated as an adjudication on the merits, thereby barring maintenance of the present action.

Dated: March 25, 2011

Respectfully submitted,

Martin J. Mushbottom
Martin J. Mushbottom
Attorney for the Defendant
657 Orchard St.
Stanford, CT 01010
(555) 555-8934
mjmushbottom@lawfirm.com

FIGURE 41: Example Motion for Summary Judgment

As with summary judgment motions, a judgment on the pleadings will be granted if the movant shows that there is no genuine issue of material fact, and that the movant is entitled to judgment as a matter of law, but there are important differences to bear in mind.

First, the time in which the two motions can be filed differs. Under the federal rules, motion for judgment on the pleadings cannot be filed until the close of pleadings, whereas a party may move for summary judgment at any time with a filing deadline set at 30 days following the close of discovery.

Most importantly, in deciding for summary judgment, the court considers all parts of the record including those obtained throughout discovery. In considering a motion for judgment on the pleadings, attack only the factual sufficiency of the pleading. With the exception of matters of public record, the court may not look beyond the pleadings and items incorporated by reference therein. Should the party raise matters outside the pleadings, and the court does not exclude them, it converts the motion to one for summary judgment and the nonmoving party must be provided an opportunity to respond.

On motions for judgment on the pleadings, courts may grant leave to amend or dismiss specific causes of action rather than grant judgment.

LEGAL MEMORANDUM

Many motions include a legal memorandum which is written to persuade the court to grant the motion. The memo goes by different names in different jurisdictions, but is most commonly referred to as a Memorandum of Points and Authorities (points because the arguments address specific points relevant to the ruling, and authorities because the arguments are based on relevant legal authority) though here, we will simply refer to it as a memo.

Typically, the more complex the motion, the more important the memo's structure becomes in ensuring the clarity and strength of the arguments. While conformance with the judge's and/or court's specifications always takes priority, the memo's structure is largely dictated by the complexity of the case and the nature of the motion it supports. A more complicated motion will typically require a memo crafted in a more structured and elaborate fashion.

A visually organized memo is easier to read, reference, and understand. Sections, divisions, and headings assist in producing the desired visual organization. You generally have some flexibility with these, with one exception: each argument in a memo should be set forth under its own point heading, and the discussion below should relate only to that argument. Features such as numbering, spacing, capitalization, underlining, italicized and boldfaced font, and other formatting options may also be utilized to produce a memo that is reader-friendly.

The components of a memo, and the order in which they are presented, will depend on its scope and length, and the court's standard practices. A basic memorandum of law is usually comprised of the following sections:

- o Caption and Title
- o Table of Contents and a Table of Authorities
- o Preliminary Statement
- o Statement of Facts
- o Points Considered (Legal Arguments)
- o Conclusion

Caption and Title

The cover page of the memo should include the case caption and the date. The memo's title should reflect the nature of both the memo itself, and the related motion. (i.e., MEMORANDUM OF POINTS AND AUTHORITIES IN SUPPORT OF/OPPOSITION TO DEFENDANT'S MOTION FOR DISMISSAL) In addition, where a request for oral argument is not provided as a separate document, it is included in the caption. (i.e., MEMORANDUM OF POINTS AND AUTHORITIES IN SUPPORT OF/OPPOSITION TO DEFENDANT'S MOTION FOR DISMISSAL AND REQUEST FOR ORAL ARGUMENT)

Table of Contents and Table of Authorities

The Table of Contents should list the first page number of all sections of the memo including all point headings and sub-headings, when applicable. Use tabs and dot leaders to line up entries and page numbers.

The Table of Authorities lists the first page number (only) on which any source of legal authority is cited in the legal arguments. Each type of authority should be listed in the table under its own heading. The order in which the headings should appear may be specified in the court rules, but typically, case law is listed first, followed by constitutional provisions, statutes, court rules and other authorities. Based on court guidelines and the judge's preference, cases may be listed in alphabetical order, or in the order by which they are cited in the memo, and statutes are listed in numerical order unless otherwise directed.

Some courts require the Tables of Contents and Authorities while others do not. For the benefit of the reader, however, it is advisable to include them in any memo exceeding 10 pages in length.

Preliminary Statement

The preliminary statement is an introduction to the memo, summarizing the legal situation and describing the reasons the motion should be granted, concisely and persuasively.

A summary of the issues and related arguments, or an outline of the positions asserted may be provided if the memo is particularly long. The preliminary statement, however, should remain brief – at most, a single page and then, only for the most extensive memos.

Although a preliminary statement outlines the legal arguments by referring to facts in the case, it contains minimal, if any, cites to case law or other materials

While a court may or may not require a preliminary statement, it serves to highlight key arguments and is, therefore, recommended.

Statement of Facts

The statement of the facts (or Factual Background) briefly describes the parties, any procedural history relevant to the motion, and a brief summary of the nature of the case. The goal of this section is to engage the attention of the judge, and to present the facts in a manner sympathetic to the client while remaining accurate and truthful.

An effective statement of facts should provide the reader with specific references to the sources of evidence which tend to prove those facts. These sources may include but are not necessarily limited to testimony, documents, witnesses, discovery responses, and affidavits. Some courts may require supporting affidavits attesting to the truth and veracity of the exhibits are true and accurate copies of what they purport to be.

Points Considered

This section constitutes the main portion of the memo, ultimately serving to connect legal precedent to the relevant facts, thus supporting the moving party's position and the propriety of the relief sought. Each argument in the memo begins with a complete sentence called a point heading. The heading is a concise summary of the argument discussed in that section and is set off from the text that follows. Point headings are entered in capital letters and are single-spaced.

The sequence of the points considered is frequently, and quite naturally, based on the rulings and elements of the law to be cited. A point is simply an affirmative phrasing of the question of law involved. A legal argument asserts a point, recounts the relevant facts, and applies legal precedent in a manner favorable to the desired outcome. A comprehensive phrasing of points will produce the strongest legal arguments. Remember that points are essentially rephrased legal issues and, like legal issues, a well-phrased point incorporates both the principle of law and existing facts directly pertinent to that principle.

As you will learn in another lesson, it is important that sources of legal authority can be easily identified and located by the reader. Rules of court generally discuss citation preferences for papers submitted to the court. If not, citations should conform to the guidelines presented in *The Bluebook*.

Conclusion

The conclusion is a short paragraph summarizing the request and the legal arguments, and specifically stating the exact relief sought. The requested relief should be clarified on a point by point basis to assist the judge in ruling on the motion. This section should be concise and direct, should summarize but not repeat, and should not introduce anything new to the reader.

ORDERS

An order is the court's decision on a motion; a proposed order is a draft of the order, as the moving party would like to have it entered, should the motion be granted. While many courts require the submission of the proposed order, it should be noted that the court is not bound by it. The proposed orders may be adopted as provided, amended to reflect the ruling, or disregarded completely. Generally, the moving party drafts the proposed order but, in some instances, the court may request that the parties collaborate.

While the court is not required to follow proposed orders, most judges find them useful as they assist in phrasing the final ruling in a manner beneficial to the party should the motion be granted. Therefore, the order should be explicit and should specify the relief to be granted.
As always, the local rules of court should be consulted to determine form, content and other orders requirements, and many judges provide their own instructions to those practicing in the court. In general, however, the order will encompass the following:

- Case caption; include case number

- Title of order:
    - Consistent with the title of the motion. For example, if filing a motion to dismiss a complaint, the proposed order is titled "Order Granting Motion to Dismiss Complaint"

- o Introductory paragraph: The introductory paragraph should state the date and time of the hearing, the name of the judge who heard the motion, the names of each attorney present and whom they represented

- o Statement of papers considered in connection with the motion, such as a supporting legal memorandum, or an affidavit

- o Findings of fact and conclusions of law, where required
  - Consistent with facts asserted in the motion, and relief requested in the motion

  - Details the court's ruling on every issue raised by the motion. In complex litigation, certain claims or defenses may be overlooked by the court, leaving portions of the case unresolved

- o Statement of specific relief granted:
  - Match the language employed in the motion's prayer for relief

  - set forth all relief granted or denied and findings where required

Many courts or judges stipulate additional requirements, such as a 3 or 4-inch top margin on the first page, or inclusion of the phrase "End of Document" centered below the last paragraph of the order, and inclusion or exclusion of the judge's signature line.

ORDER vs. JUDGMENT

It is important to distinguish between orders and judgments. Generally, a judgment is the final decision rendered by the court and constitutes the ultimate resolution or outcome of the litigated case. A judgment declares the winning party, specifies the relief granted to the winning party and obligations imposed upon the losing party. A judgment is always in writing and issued and signed by the judge.

Conversely, orders are preliminary directives issued by the judge to resolve interim disputes between the parties. Orders do not resolve the ultimate issue or issues upon which the litigation is based, nor do they constitute the ultimate outcome of said litigation. As discussed above, orders are commonly drafted and proposed by a party to the case, and the decision to rule accordingly is at the discretion of the court.

It should be noted that some interim judgments may not ultimately dispose of the entire legal matter. Motions for summary or default judgment, for instance, frequently result in an "interlocutory" judgment which may dispose of only some parties and/or issues in the case, leaving others to proceed with litigation.

Caption omitted

ORDER GRANTING PLAINTIFF'S MOTION

FOR LEAVE TO AMEND COMPLAINT

This cause came on for hearing on the motion of Plaintiff under Rule 15(a) (2) of the Rules of Civil Procedure, for an order allowing Plaintiff to amend her complaint in this action, and it appears to the court that plaintiff has demonstrated that good cause exists and justice requires the grant of leave to file the proposed amended complaint.

Therefore, Plaintiff's Motion is GRANTED

SO ORDERED, this ____ day of _____

Judgely C. DoRight

Hon. Judgely C. DoRight
U.S. District Court Judge

FIGURE 42: Example Order

AMENDED & SUPPLEMENTAL PLEADINGS (FRCP 15)

State and federal rules of civil procedure make allowances when pleadings need to be amended or supplemented. Amended pleadings involve matters which occurred prior to the filing of the original pleading. Supplemental pleadings, on the other hand, deal with events occurring after the initial pleading was filed, and present additions to or continuations of that earlier pleading.

Amended Pleadings

FRCP 15(a) grants a party the right to file one amended pleading at any time before a responsive pleading is served, or if the pleading is one to which no responsive pleading is permitted and the court has not yet docketed the case. Otherwise, a party may amend a pleading only by leave of court or by written consent of the opposing party.

When preparing an amended pleading, it is important to bear in mind that, in essence, the amendment completely replaces the initially filed pleading, and the original no longer performs any function in the case. While it is permissible to adopt by reference statements from the initial pleading, it is best if the amended pleading is complete in itself, thus avoiding the need to constantly refer to the original. If, for some reason, the supervising attorney prefers to incorporate prior allegations, they must be clearly, directly and explicitly identified.

Unless otherwise ordered by the court, the response to an amended pleading is due within the time remaining for response to the original, or within 14 days after service of the amended pleading, whichever is longer.

Supplemental Pleadings

Under FRCP 15(d), a court may permit a party to serve supplemental pleadings to bring the case up to date. Unlike an amended pleading, the supplemental pleading does not replace the original. Instead, the supplement merely continues the earlier pleading and they are treated as a one. Therefore, it is important to avoid supplemental pleadings in which the legal conflict involves allegations substantially different than those posed in the initial pleading.

The filing of a supplemental pleading is not a matter of right. Leave to file must be granted by the court upon reasonable notice and must be sought by motion. *See Figure 43 for an example motion to amend the pleadings.*

A response to a supplemental pleading may or may not be required depending on the nature of the supplement. If a response is required, the court will order the opposing party to reply within a specified time.

Pleadings and motions are important in any legal matter. They serve to initiate the claim, to support the client's case, to communicate with the courts as well as opposing counsel, and will be referenced repeatedly throughout the case. Generally, you can obtain everything you'll need regarding form and procedure through your court rules and various forms sources, but your best resource for effectively drafting these documents will likely be your supervising attorney. Be sure to understand the nature of any assigned drafting task and to seek clarification on anything you may not fully understand. As many attorneys say: the strength of a case often lies in the strength of its pleadings.

A note on E-filing

By Margaret J. Kirk, ACP

E-filing, or filing documents with a court electronically, has become widely accepted by State and Federal Courts. Some states have made e-filing mandatory for specific courts. E-filing saves time and paper, and offers convenient access to the court at any time, but e-filing is not entirely paperless. Documents are filed with electronic signatures, and most courts require that an original paper document with actual signatures be kept by the filer. It is very important to print and keep the "receipt" issued by the court for the document that was filed electronically. It may become necessary to prove that a document was filed and accepted by a court on a specific day at a specific time.

Much like filing paper documents with any court, courts have specific rules regarding formatting, types of files that may be used for sending documents and limits to the size of the documents filed. Generally courts want documents sent in .pdf format. However, it is very important to check the local rules of the specific court before attempting to file a document electronically. Courts that do allow or mandate electronic filing of documents have their own websites with specific instructions for electronic filing. An Internet search for a specific court should provide a link to electronic filing information for that court, or you can contact your local court clerk for more information.

When a document is filed electronically, service of the document must be made to certain parties just as with filing a paper document with a court. For example, if service is made electronically in a Federal civil proceeding under the Federal Rules of Civil Procedure, three days must be added to the time allowed for a response (if one is required). [Fed. R. Civ. P. Rule 6(d)] It is important to check individual State Rules of Procedure to determine the number of days, if any, that must be added for electronic service in a State Court proceeding.

CM/ECF (Case Management/Electronic Case Files) is the system used for filing documents electronically for Federal Courts, and may be accessed through PACER (Public Access to Court Electronic Records) online at http://PACER.gov. The website contains information on how to navigate the site, as well as how to file and access documents. PACER also provides access to Federal Appellate Court, U.S. District Court, and Bankruptcy Court case and docket information. In order to use PACER, a log-in and password must be created. Credit card or other billing information is also required.

There are minimal fees for viewing and printing documents on PACER. For example, case documents and docket sheets are $0.10 per page. PACER's website contains a schedule of fees, so that the cost of document retrieval can be estimated in advance. When filing a document that requires a filing fee, a credit card is used to pay the fee.

While information retrieved on PACER is not free, it is certainly cheaper than spending time and money to travel to a court house in search of documents. Instant access to documents filed with courts, and the ability to file documents with courts evenings, weekends, and holidays, has made the process of retrieving information and filing documents much more efficient and convenient.

CHAPTER FOUR: DISCOVERY

Jolie R. Kulsar

Discovery is the formal process of exchanging information between the parties about the witnesses and evidence they'll present at trial. Discovery narrows the issues involved in a lawsuit, allows parties to obtain evidence for use at trial, and brings to light information that might be introduced as evidence at trial. Granting parties access to material facts not protected by privilege facilitates a fair trial, and frequently, results in a settlement agreement which ends litigation without the need for trial.

A party to litigation is generally entitled to the production and inspection of relevant documents in the possession or control of an adversary pursuant to discovery. The requesting party must have a reasonable belief that such evidence is necessary to the lawsuit if discovery is to be granted. Material that is considered non-discoverable, such as confidential, or privileged information, or material prepared in anticipation of litigation (work product) need not be turned over to the opposition unless directed to do so by court order. A court will halt discovery not conducted in good faith. Federal and State Rules of Civil procedure specify the allowable methods of discovery. Common discovery devices include:

Deposition

A deposition is a proceeding in which a witness or party is asked to answer questions orally under oath before a court reporter. A deponent can be deposed orally, or upon written questions.

- **Oral Depositions** –After an action has been commenced, any party may take the oral testimony of any person thought to have information within the scope of discovery. This is known as an oral deposition. Not only parties, but any non-party with relevant information, may be deposed. If a non-party is to be deposed, then the discovering party can only force the deponent to attend by issuing a subpoena. The subpoena must require the deposition to be held no more than 100 miles from the place where the deponent resides, is employed, or regularly transacts business in person. The party ordering the deposition can arrange to have it recorded by stenography (court reporter), by audio tape recorder, or by video recorder.

- **Depositions upon Written Questions**: Any party may take the responses to written questions, from any person (party or non-party) thought to have discoverable information. This is called a "deposition on written questions." Depositions on written questions are mainly used for deposing distant non-party witnesses. Such witnesses cannot be served with interrogatories (since these are limited to parties), and cannot be compelled to travel more than 100 miles from their home or business. Written depositions may be completed and attested to before a notary or other authorized officer of the court.

Once the date and time of the deposition has been established, the attorney must file the Notice of Taking Deposition with the court and provide copies to all parties and the court reporter. *See Figure 44.*

Subpoena

A subpoena is an order telling a witness to appear in court or at a deposition. A subpoena is issued by the court, and if the witness fails to comply, he can be held in contempt of court. "Subpoena" in Latin means "under penalty".

Subpoena duces tecum

Subpoena *duces tecum* is an order telling a witness to turn over certain documents to a specific party or to bring them to a scheduled deposition. A subpoena *duces tecum* is issued by the court, and if the witness fails to comply, he can be held in contempt. *See Figure 45 for an example subpoena.*

Interrogatories

Interrogatories are written questions sent by one party to the other party for the latter to answer in writing under oath. Interrogatories may be addressed only to a party. *See Appendix C for example interrogatories.*

Request for admission

One party sends the other a request for admission; that he admit certain facts. The purpose of a request for admission is to find areas of agreement and limit the contested areas at trial. The other party is asked to admit to certain facts. Probably she will not do so, but to the extent that there is agreement, these facts can be stipulated and not argued at trial. *See Figure 9 in Chapter One for an example body of a request for admissions. A complete request for admissions is located in Appendix D.*

***Request for physical and mental examination*--**a request to a party that he be examined by a doctor if his health or mental condition is at issue. This is particularly important in personal injury cases. A defendant's insurance provider will often require the plaintiff to be examined by a doctor of its choosing. This is known as an independent medical examination.

IN THE CIRCUIT COURT OF LAKE COUNTY, ILLINOIS
Municipal Department, Nineteenth Judicial District

Fea Fifofum,)
)
Plaintiff,)
)
-vs-)   NO.   **CD-1122-9425-11**
)
Winken B. Nodd,)
)
Defendant.)

NOTICE OF DEPOSITION

TO:Milford J. Munny
000 Park Avenue
Suite B
Chicago, IL 55551

YOU ARE HEREBY NOTIFIED that pursuant to the applicable rules of the Illinois Supreme Court, the deposition of the Plaintiff, Fea Fifofum will be taken for the purposes of discovery only on July 7, 2011, at 9:00 a.m. at the Law Offices of Reba L. Withacauz upon oral interrogatories to be propounded to said deponent, before a Notary Public in and for the County of Lake, State of Illinois, at which time and place you are requested to present said deponent.

Deponent is to bring with Deponent any and all:

1. Books, records, correspondence with Defendant or third parties, and any and all other documents related to the premises occupied by Defendant and the purported reason or reasons for plaintiffs filing the within lawsuit against Defendant.

2. All books and records, leases, applications for a lease, contracts, receipts, correspondence or notes of any kind or nature whatsoever that is not protected by the attorney-client relationship, related, directly or indirectly, to the matters alleged in Plaintiff's complaint and Defendant's answer, affirmative defense(s) and counterclaim(s).

3. Any and all records relating to the receipt of rentals and the payment of interest on security deposits of Defendant.

4. Any and all correspondence of any kind or nature whatsoever with the City of Chicago

FIGURE 44: Example Notice of Deposition

Building Department and any administrative agencies of the City of Chicago in regard thereto.

5. Any and all correspondence with Defendant, Counterplaintiff, during the term of any lease or leases between the parties.

6. Repair estimates, vouchers, cancelled checks, estimates from vendors, vendors= bills and statements and any and all other documents related to the premises in question for the entire time Defendant has been Plaintiff's tenant.

7. The contract for the purchase or other acquisition of the real estate and the sale of the real estate in which the tenant leases an apartment, and any and all amendments and attachments thereto.

8. Any and all escrow agreements, closing statements, assignments of leases, contracts, undertakings or other documents related to the acquisition or purchase or sale of the property in which the tenant occupies an apartment, whether with the mortgage company or mortgage companies who have been involved with mortgages or the financing of the premises in question.

9. Any and all correspondence with any of the mortgage holders as to the building in question.

Dated: June 1, 2011

Reba L. Withacauz
Reba L. Withacauz
Attorney for Defendant

CERTIFICATE OF DELIVERY

Under penalties as provided by law pursuant to 735 ILCS 5/1-109 of the Code of Civil Procedure, the undersigned attorney for Defendant, certify that I caused a copy of the foregoing **NOTICE OF DEPOSITION** to be delivered to the Plaintiff, in open court on June 5, 2011, by personally handing it to the Plaintiff.

Reba L. Withacauz
Reba L. Withacauz
         Counsel For Defendant

Reba L. Withacauz,
Counsel for Defendant
9001 E. South St. – Ste. #17
Chicago, IL 60611
(555) 555-5554
Atty. No. 00990

FIGURE 44: Example Notice of Deposition continued

AO 88A (Rev. 06/09) Subpoena to Testify at a Deposition in a Civil Action

UNITED STATES DISTRICT COURT
for the
Southern District of Florida

Cornelius Furbis III	)
Plaintiff	)
v.	) Civil Action No. 844-ZZ-606D-12
Mary L. Poppins	)
	) (If the action is pending in another district, state where:
Defendant	))

SUBPOENA TO TESTIFY AT A DEPOSITION IN A CIVIL ACTION

To: Rickard B. Pigg

☒ *Testimony:* **YOU ARE COMMANDED** to appear at the time, date, and place set forth below to testify at a deposition to be taken in this civil action. If you are an organization that is *not* a party in this case, you must designate one or more officers, directors, or managing agents, or designate other persons who consent to testify on your behalf about the following matters, or those set forth in an attachment:

Place: Law Offices of Dewey, Cheatum and Howe
        999 Clifford Vale
        Simeon, Florida 00610
	Date and Time: 02/09/2013 2:00 p.m.

The deposition will be recorded via this method: Video Recording and Transcription

☒   *Production:* You, or your representatives, must also bring with you to the deposition the following documents, electronically stored information, or objects, and permit their inspection, copying, testing, or sampling of the material:

Any and all photographs in your possession of the above-named parties to the suit Any and all diaries in your possession mentioning the above-named parties to the suit Any and all writings under your authorship regarding the above-named parties to the suit

The provisions of Fed. R. Civ. P. 45(c), relating to your protection as a person subject to a subpoena, and Rule 45 (d) and (e), relating to your duty to respond to this subpoena and the potential consequences of not doing so, are attached.

Date: 12/15/2012

CLERK OF COURT

OR

_____   _____
Signature of Clerk or Deputy Clerk   *Attorney's signature*

The name, address, e-mail, and phone number of the attorney representing *(name of party):* Cornelius Furbus III

_____ , who issues or requests this subpoena, are:

James Strongworth Dewey
9999 Clifford Vale
Simeon, Florida 00610   jsd@dchlegal.com

FIGURE 45: Example Federal Subpoena

***Request for production of documents*--**a request to a party to hand over certain defined documents. In family law cases, parties often request from each other bank statements, pay stubs and other documents showing earnings, assets and debts. Unless there is objection made to the court on the grounds that this is privileged information, the opposing party is required to comply with this request. *See Figure 46 for an example body of a request for production of documents. Appendix E also contains an example request for production of documents.*

Caption omitted

Pursuant to § 2031 of the New York Code of Civil Procedure, Plaintiffs, by and through their attorneys, hereby demand that the Defendant produce for discovery, inspecting and copying at the Law Offices of Smith, Browne and Jones, 100 First Avenue, Buffalo, New York, 00000, the following documents and material.

INSTRUCTIONS

(Omitted For Example Purposes)

DOCUMENTS TO BE PRODUCED

1. Provide legible copies of each insurance policy for Polly Kettle's Tea Emporium.

2. Provide all photographs, videotapes or audio tapes, x-rays, diagrams, surveys or other graphic representations of information concerning the subject matter of this action, the Plaintiff, or property damage.

FIGURE 46: Example body of request for production

***Request for inspection*--**a request by a party to look at tangible items (other than writings) in the possession or control of the other party. Items to be inspected include houses, cars, appliances and virtually any other physical item.

***Request to Enter Land*--**If the place where the incident occurred is not on public property, the gathering of evidence or the viewing of the scene is important to your case. In that instance, you must be authorized to go upon the land and see where it happened, and what other explanation might account for the injury or loss.

The scope of information obtainable through discovery is quite broad and not limited to what can be used in a trial. Federal courts and most state courts allow a party to discover any information "reasonably calculated to lead to the discovery of admissible evidence." Because of this broad standard, parties often disagree about what information must be exchanged and what may be kept confidential. These disputes are resolved through court rulings on discovery motions.

Discovery generally follows the form of pleadings, including the case caption and title (e.g., Request for Admissions). The body of the document is formatted in chronologically numbered paragraphs, which are double-spaced, and sufficient space is left in which the answer can be provided. A signature line for the responding party is provided along with a certificate of service. Discovery must generally be notarized.

The discovery process has long been the source of much of the time, stress, and costs involved in litigation. Document production and inspection has always involved the need to review, organize, categorize, digest and analyze the materials produced. This need remains in the electronic age, but adds new issues to the process. While electronic document production and preservation saves the law practice from receiving stacks upon stacks of papers, the ease with which electronic documents can be modified or deleted completely, poses special problems and imposes special ethical practices. To further complicate these issues, most business practices commonly result in a cycle of document management which includes the regular destruction, or storage of documents in ways that render them difficult to access.

E-DISCOVERY

Electronic discovery (e-discovery) is the process of preserving, collecting and filtering ESI (electronically stored information) for relevant information which must then be provided to the requesting party for use in litigation.

Electronic discovery is not at issue in all cases, such as those where the parties agree to simply exchange traditional paper documents, or those in which the amount in controversy does not justify the significant costs that can be involved in producing ESI.

In others, such as those involving copyright infringement or other intellectual property issues, for example, compelling ESI may form the basis of the matter, or provide proof or disproof of conduct inherent to the claim to such an extent that the time and financial burden is warranted. Most cases, however, will likely involve e-discovery to at least some extent. In those instances, the parties have a duty to fulfill certain obligations in requesting and producing discoverable ESI, including the duty to protect relevant ESI, the duty to identify and locate relevant ESI, the duty to collect and preserve relevant ESI, and the duty to produce relevant ESI.

The Duty to Protect

Many businesses are required to maintain records for a specified period of time as a regular business practice. Certain financial records, employment records, contracts and transaction records related to an industry are generally maintained until enough time has passed to ensure that the records can safely be destroyed.

Court decisions and rules of civil procedure impose upon public and private entities a legal duty to preserve electronic materials and records that might be relevant to pending or anticipated litigation. Once a client has reason to believe that the possibility of a lawsuit exists, good faith efforts must be made to protect and preserve relevant electronic information from destruction and manipulation, which may be the result of regular document management policies, or attempts to avoid incrimination.

A litigation hold is a stipulation dictating the need to cease any and all activity which may result in the destruction or modification of relevant files. Events triggering a litigation hold can be as ambiguous as what appears at face value to be an idle threat to sue, or as concrete as service of a summons and complaint, or receipt of a preservation letter from a party/party's counsel in a potential lawsuit. While modification to ESI prior to a triggering event is acceptable, absolutely no modification is permissible once a complaint has been filed, or a preservation letter received.

A preservation letter informs a potential party to litigation of the nature of the dispute, the identity of individuals or departments involved, and relevant dates. This is not a discovery instrument, but rather, a request that the party avoid deleting, destroying or modifying specific, or general categories of, relevant ESI. In addition, the suspension of regular document retention procedures and an acknowledgment is requested.

All employees, record keepers and IT personnel must be informed of the litigation hold and materials must be preserved without further modification or destruction. The destruction of, or failure to preserve, discoverable data by a party to litigation is called spoliation and is punishable by sanctions. Hence, effective, thorough and ethical compliance requires the cooperative efforts of attorneys, IT departments, management, and employees involved in creating or maintaining any of the relevant records. The party may be called upon to verify compliance with the obligations imposed by a litigation hold, so cooperation should be carefully monitored, and thorough records should be maintained.

The Duty to Identify and Locate

Records relevant to the lawsuit must be identified and preserved, so that they cannot be altered, and can be collected for further review. Attorneys may agree upon the methods to be used in determining relevancy in what is known as a "meet and confer" session (FRCP 26[f]) – which is a mandatory, cooperative meeting to discuss the scope and limitations of discovery. Relevant data may include correspondence, including e-mails, voicemails and instant messages; payment or financial records, including spreadsheet data; any word processing documents containing evidence, etc.

Parties do not have a duty to disclose confidential or privileged information, data that is created in preparation for a lawsuit (work-product), or information that is not relevant to the case, or likely to lead to information that is relevant to the case. In addition, ESI that is not reasonably accessible may also be considered non-discoverable, depending on its relevance, the cost in rendering it accessible, the agreements reached by the attorneys and, in some instances, a ruling by the court.

Specific individuals likely to be involved in the creation, modification and/or maintenance of records, as well as those likely to have relevant records in their possession, or to have knowledge of where such records might be created and/or stored, must then be identified. Staff undertaking duties specific to the party or matter involved are likely to possess relevant data, as are the immediate supervisor for that staff member. Department heads, outside contractors and consultants who may have been involved in the matter should also be interviewed, as well as those involved in records management or maintenance. Depending on the size, structure and type of the business, this list can be quite extensive. Again, it is important that this process be documented and treated as an ongoing obligation throughout the discovery process.

The various types of ESI which may have been created must also be fully considered. Documentation, such as contracts or correspondence may have been created using word processing applications, but saved as .pdf files; payroll and financial information may exist as spreadsheets; relevant dates and other information may be contained in a database; and presentations may have been prepared using PowerPoint, or another presentation graphics program. In addition, businesses can send and receive thousands of emails each month, and even voicemail messages can be the source of important information. Each of these, as well as other types of data, must be identified, located, protected and reviewed.

Once data creators and custodians have been identified, all data sources must then be considered. Obviously, the computers of anyone potentially involved in creating or maintaining documents relevant to the matter will be of interest, as will the organization's network. The assistance of IT staff, network administrators and others involved in data storage and management must be enlisted to construct a data map, which details the data management policies, structure and directories. Relevant ESI must be collected from all sources, including messaging archives, back up data systems, file servers, desktops, laptops, staff home computers, flash and jump drives, PDA's and smart phones, etc...

The Duty to Collect and Preserve

Files containing potentially discoverable information are then collected for indexing and processing. Specific software is generally required, and e-discovery service providers are usually brought in to perform this function, as the integrity and quality of the ESI must be maintained. The time investment can be high, and experience and competence provides an extra measure of security and credibility in the eyes of the court. A service provider has the resources, tools and methods to organize, manage and process collected data, maintain and generate reports and documentation, and can serve as witness to correct and ethical procedures, if necessary.

Collected data must be reviewed in a format that can be searched effectively, in order to produce all relevant and discoverable information. This process, referred to as "culling" allows for the removal of duplicates, and the redaction of privileged or confidential information, and begins with entering all of the original data into a unified, comprehensive database, which can be fully indexed and is designed for large-scale searching and review formats.

Files are then converted into common, viewable formats, such as PDF, TIFF or HTML while access to the native file is maintained with all metadata intact. ESI is filtered and reviewed through multiple searches, commonly utilizing a web-based review tool. Searches might involve date, author, file-type, key word and even conceptual searches, which will locate related terms similar to a thesaurus. Again, documentation of search criteria, sampling methods and proper indexing is important for both organization and for presentation to the court, if necessary.

The Duty to Produce

Data production can be complex and problems may be encountered. Hence, each page should be Bates stamped for unique identification, easy access and quick reference. This is easily automated for scanned TIFF or PDF files, and some software programs allow for Bates numbering at both the page level, for PDF documents, and at the file name level for native file documents. Designations of confidential and 'attorneys' eyes only' are also included in the Bates stamp, as appropriate.

Upon the final filtering and review relevant, non-privileged, discoverable ESI must be turned over to the requesting party. This information also provides the attorney for the producing party with a comprehensive picture of much of the evidence involved in the case. The file format in which the final data set is provided is frequently determined at the meet and confer session, and the information is generally saved and accessed through CD-Roms, DVD's, or hosted servers.

Conclusion

Electronic discovery is one of the most prominent issues confronting the legal industry today. As amended in 2006, the Federal Rules of Civil Procedure confer tremendous responsibility upon attorneys involved in litigation entailing electronic discovery. E-discovery service providers are frequently brought in to manage all aspects of e-discovery, but attorneys remain responsible for overseeing the process and its results. State and local chapters of the Bar Association, as well as continuing education seminars designed for legal staff are good resources for those interested in learning more about their roles in electronic discovery.

Chapter Five: Appellate Procedure

William E. Thoms, Professor Emeritus of Law, University of North Dakota

An appeal is a petition to a higher court to examine the record of a court below, and to set aside or change the lower court's decision on the grounds that error has occurred at the trial level. The person initiating the appeal is the appellant; the appellee is the party against whom the appeal is filed. In some jurisdictions, they are referred to as petitioner and respondent, respectively.

For a long time, Connecticut's highest court was called the Supreme Court of Errors, which was a cause of a good deal of humor among the bar of that state. It was accurate, however. An appeals court exists to reverse or cure any error made in the trial. Since a jury trial makes the jury the arbiter of the facts (which is not subject to appeal), an appeal to a higher court states that the judge committed some error of law.

> In Louisiana, which has its own unique civil law system, the Court of Appeals can also review errors of fact.

The error may be in the judge's charge to the jury, telling them what is applicable law, or, more likely, an error in admitting certain exhibits, witnesses, or testimony. An appeal is made to a higher court alleging that the lower court committed an error.

THE APPELLATE PROCESS

The first thing your principal lawyer should do is order and examine a copy of the record of trial. The record consists of the case docket, transcripts of the proceedings, exhibits, pleadings, motions and briefs. The transcript should be read carefully, to locate any material errors in the proceedings. A material error is such a grievous matter that it unfairly influenced the wrongful outcome of the trial. Often such an instance is called "reversible error." That means that the court proceeded so erroneously that the decision of the trial court should be reversed. To begin the appeal, your office should serve a notice of appeal on the opposing party, stating that your client intends to appeal the decision to a higher court. (*See Figure 47*) This puts your opponent on notice that an appeal will be filed and he will be timely served with your brief, to which he is expected to reply.

> *Please note that all examples are for instructional purposes only. They may not show the proper formatting requirements for your jurisdiction. Always check your local appellate rules for format specifications.*

UNITED STATES DISTRICT COURT

FOR THE NORTHERN DISTRICT OF FICTION

MARCIA HANSON;

     Plaintiff,

           v.   File No. 12-35798

JOHN and RITA SMART,

     Defendant,

NOTICE OF APPEAL

Notice is hereby given that Marcia Hanson, plaintiff in the above named case, hereby appeals to the United States Court of Appeals for the Tenth Circuit from the final judgment entered in this action on month, day, year.

_____

Some Lawyer

Attorney for Plaintiff

4567 Any Lane

Anytown, Fiction 37214

Dated: _____

FIGURE 47: Notice of Appeal

THE APPELLATE BRIEF

There are neither witnesses nor sworn testimony in appeals. No new evidence will be heard; hence it will be limited to the issues presented at the trial court level. Therefore, success and victory depends upon oral argument and the strength of your brief. Every argument that you intend to make should be included in the brief. You must assume the appellate judges will have read the brief before the oral presentation is given. But the attorney may well have to repeat many things in his argument before the appeals court.

The appellate brief should contain as much factual information as you can gather to buttress your argument. The brief format is structured similarly in both state and federal courts. However, it is imperative that you always check your appellate rules before beginning your brief. The usual arrangement for the preparation of an appeal brief is as follows:

Cover Page - The cover page should include identification of the parties, case number assigned, name of the lower court, brief title, and the court to which the appeal is sent. You may also need to include the attorney's name and contact information. (*See Figure 50*)

Table of contents - Every part of the brief should be referred to by the correct page on which it is found. (*See Figure 48*)

TABLE OF CONTENTS

Index of Authorities X

Statement of Jurisdiction X

Statement of Issues X

Statement of Facts X

Argument X

Conclusion X

Relief X

FIGURE 48: Example Table of Contents

Index of authorities - If case law, statutes, or even law review articles are cited, they should appear in this section where they are accessible at a glance. Cases should be listed alphabetically and statutes should be listed in the order in which they appear in the brief. (*See Figure 49*)

INDEX OF AUTHORITIES

Cases

Party A v. Party B, _ _ XX _ _ _ (Fict. 199_)

You v. Me, _ _ _ XX.2d _ _ (Fict. 197_)

Statutes

Fiction State Statute § XX-X-XXX

FIGURE 49: Example Index of Authorities

IN THE

COURT OF APPEALS OF THE STATE OF FICTION

No. 00-00001

MARCIA HANSON,

Petitioner,

v.

JOHN and RITA SMART,

Respondent.

ON APPEAL TO THE COURT OF APPEALS OF

THE STATE OF FICTION FROM

THE FICTITIOUS TRIAL COURT

BRIEF OF PETITIONER

Some Lawyer

Attorney for Petitioner

4567 Any Lane

Anytown, Fiction 37214

FIGURE 50: Example cover page

Statement of jurisdiction - This is a simple statement asserting the court's jurisdiction over the persons and matters that are pertinent to the case. (*See Figure 51*)

STATEMENT OF JURISDICTION

This Honorable Court has jurisdiction pursuant to Fiction Code Annotated § xx-x-xxx

---

FIGURE 51: Example Statement of Jurisdiction

Statement of issues - This is sometimes referred to as "Statement of Questions Presented". Here is where you define what you want the court to consider. Usually the appellant will state questions as to what constitutes reversible error by the court below. (*See Figure 52*)

QUESTIONS PRESENTED

DOES Fiction State Statute § XX-X-XXX PROVIDE FOR A DISMISSAL BASED ON A FIRST BITE DEFFENSE?

FIGURE 52: Example statement of the issues

Statement of facts – This may also be referred to as "Statement of the Case". Since you are appealing only the court's statement of the law, this should be straightforward. The facts of the case include who the parties are and how the dispute arose. It may also include a statement of the lower court's proceedings and a summary of the lower court's decision. *(See Figure 53)*

Argument - This is the main portion of the brief. After stating the facts, you begin to develop the argument. Each point that you are making should have a separate paragraph, with a topic sentence followed by as many explanatory sentences as it takes to explain why the court below erred. Here each point you make should be followed by a reference to the applicable authority. (*See Figure 56*)

Conclusion - State what the court should certainly conclude after listening to your terrific arguments in favor of the proposition. Sum it up with one sentence, which should lead you to the next part, relief. (*See Figure 54*)

STATEMENT OF THE FACTS

On April 23, 2008, at approximately 4:00 AM, Marcia Hanson was delivering newspapers for The Smalltown newspaper in Anytown, Fiction. As Ms. Hanson approached the home of John & RITA SMART, their dog, a male pit bull named Spot, ran barking from the back of the house and approached Ms. Hanson on the sidewalk. Spot then charged Ms. Hanson, biting her on the right leg, ankle and foot. Mrs. SMART unsuccessfully attempted to call Spot off of Ms. Hanson. Hearing the commotion, Mr. SMART came out of the house and commanded Spot to "hold down," at which time the dog immediately released Ms. Hanson's foot and ran to Mr. SMART. Mrs. SMART called 911 and within minutes the Anytown Fire Department and paramedics arrived at the scene. They staunched the flow of blood from Ms. Hanson's foot and transported her to Smalltown Hospital where she was sedated and received 140 stitches in her right leg, ankle and foot. She was given a tetanus shot and admitted for overnight observation.

Smalltown Police Department arrived at the scene where they took a report from Mr. & Mrs. SMART, recorded Spot's rabies number, and informed them that Spot would have to be impounded for 10 days as required by county ordinance. The SMART's informed the police that they would take Spot to their veterinarian for the period of impoundment. The police attempted to interview Ms. Hanson at the hospital, but she was heavily sedated and could not speak at the time.

Trial was held in Fictitious Trial Court on December 19th, 2008, Honorable Judge Noble Judge presiding. Judge Judge ruled that while Ms. Hanson was in fact bitten by Spot and was required to have 140 stitches, the Defendant's would not be held liable under the "first bite" doctrine. The first bite rule exempts dog owners from liability for damages incurred if the dog has not previously bitten

FIGURE 53: Example statement of facts

CONCLUSION

The trial court erred in dismissing Ms. Hanson's claim for damages. The SMART's are liable for not keeping the animal under their control and allowing it to run at large which resulted in harm to the Petitioner, Marcia Hanson.

FIGURE 54: Example conclusion

Relief - Also called "Prayer for Relief." Here is where you ask the court what you want it to do, which amounts to either substituting its judgment for that of the court below, or remanding it to the lower court to correct its previous error. (*See Figure 55*)

RELIEF

WHEREFORE, Petitioner respectfully requests that this Honorable Court reverse the decision of the Trial Court and award Ms. Marcia Hanson all medical bills, lost wages, and pain and suffering in the amount of $150,000.00.

FIGURE 55: Example prayer for relief

Appendix - Here you put all the relevant procedural documents from the lower court: explanatory material, including a bibliography, citations and references to the exhibits used at trial.

ARGUMENT

A DOG OWNER WHO IGNORES THE DUTY TO KEEP THE DOG UNDER CONTROL IS LIABLE FOR DAMAGES TO SOMEONE WHO IS NOT TRESPASSING.

Fiction State Statute§ XX-X-XXX – Injury caused by dogs; civil liability; exceptions; limitations provides the following in part:

> *(1)(a) The owner of a dog has a duty to keep that dog under reasonable control at all times, and to keep that dog from running at large. A person who breaches that duty is subject to civil liability for any damages suffered by a person who is injured by the dog while in a public place or lawfully in or on the private property of another.*

> *(1)(b)* The owner may be held liable regardless of whether the dog has shown any dangerous propensities or whether the dog's owner knew or should have known of the dog's dangerous propensities.

> *(2) Subsection (1) shall not impose liability upon the owner of the dog if:*

> *(2) (b) The injured person was trespassing on the property of the dog's owner.*

Pursuant to the above, the owner of a dog has a duty to keep that dog under reasonable control at all times. Neither Mr. nor Mrs. SMART had Spot under their control, as evidenced by the fact that he was able to reach Ms. Hanson at the sidewalk before she had even crossed the property line. If the dog was unleashed, it can be considered "at large." Subsection (1)(b) also clearly states that the owner will be held liable regardless of any dangerous propensities, known or unknown, thus invalidating any first bite provisions.

FIGURE 56: Example argument section

MOTIONS ON APPEAL

Federal and state rules of civil and criminal procedure require that a court be moved to examine a petition and make certain changes or grant certain requests. An appellate court is not entitled to take notice or to give relief *sua sponte* (on its own initiative). Therefore, a request for procedural changes, interim orders, awarding of costs or emergency relief must be brought to the notice of the court in a motion. Your opponent must be then given time to reply to your motions.

Motion for extension of time - In some states this may be called motion for enlargement of time. This is a plea for the court to consider exigent circumstances, and to either allow more time to respond to the opponent's brief or to delay a particular deadline. You should be very specific about why this extension or delay is necessary for the presentation of the case.

Procedural orders - These are motions for the court to issue orders regarding the handling of the appeal. Here, again, specificity is vital. Explain clearly to the court how your office's client would like the appeal to be handled and why his request is justified for the expeditious handling of the case.

Costs - This is a motion for costs to be awarded to your client. The rationale is that the erroneous decision below has burdened your client with additional costs and she should be compensated for the extra expenditures.

Emergency relief - This is a request for an order to stop or prevent irreparable damage. Usually the motion will call for an injunction or a temporary restraining order to prevent the other side from doing something that would drastically harm your client's position.

Appellate practice is distinctly different from litigation practice. Professional emphasis for the appellate paralegal will be on research, writing, and maintaining familiarity with advanced concepts in jurisprudence. The main function of an appellate brief is to convince higher courts to substitute their judgment for that of lower trial courts. Trial judges do not like to be reversed on appeal, and they therefore write their opinions to be as persuasive as possible. The appellate brief must counter these typically well-written opinions. Paralegals going into this type of work should have a strong inclination toward research and great organization skills to handle the massive amount of paperwork that is inherent in appellate practice.

APPENDIX A:

A COMPLAINT

 THE CENTER FOR LEGAL STUDIES

IN THE UNITED STATES DISTRICT COURT FOR THE EASTERN DISTRICT OF NEW YORK

SANFORD & SONS LIMITED,
a Swiss Corporation,

Plaintiff,	
v.	NO. _____

CAC AVIATION CORPORATION
a New York Corporation,

Defendant.

COMPLAINT FOR BREACH OF CONTRACT, UNJUST ENRICHMENT, AND CONVERSION WITH JURY TRIAL

For its complaint Plaintiff, SANFORD & SONS Limited, states as follows:

I.   THE PARTIES AND JURISDICTION

1.   Plaintiff, SANFORD & SONS Limited, ("S&S"), is a limited company, organized under Swiss law, having its principal place of business in Berne, Switzerland.

2.   Defendant, CAC Aviation Corporation ("CAC") is a corporation, organized under New York law, having its principal place of business in Hamburg, New York.

3.   CAC may be served with process by serving its registered agent: Mr.

Thomas Schultz, 9276 Stickford Avenue, Hamburg, NY 01000.

4.   Jurisdiction is proper in this court pursuant to 28 U.S.C. § 1332, because the

plaintiff is a resident of a foreign country, and the defendant is a corporation incorporated

under the laws of the State of New York, with its principal place of business in the State of

New York. The amount in controversy, without interest, costs or attorneys' fees, exceeds

the amount specified by 28 U.S.C. § 1332.

II.   FACTS

5.   On or about November 26, 2010, S&S and CAC entered into a CAC 500

Aircraft Deposit Agreement (the "Deposit Agreement") relating to the sale and delivery, on

one hand, and the purchase, on the other hand, of a CAC S-730 model aircraft, for the

Standard Aircraft Price amount of $1,520,000, exclusive of optional equipment, and as

adjusted pursuant to an economic escalation formula.

6.   As relevant to the matters contained in this complaint, the Deposit

Agreement provides that S&S, as the buyer, would make an initial deposit of $25,000,

followed by a series of pre-delivery payments and additional deposits, as follows: (1)

$75,000 six (6) months after execution of the Deposit Agreement; and (2) $80,000 twelve

(12) months after execution of the Deposit Agreement; and (3) up to sixty percent (60%) of

the total amount six (6) months prior to scheduled delivery of the aircraft; and (4)

unpaid balance, due at delivery.

7.   The Deposit Agreement provides that the pre-delivery payments and deposits

are refundable following the occurrence of a "Refund Event," defined in the agreement

to include, among other things, an increase in the Standard Aircraft Price for reasons other

than the economic escalation formula.

2

8.   The Deposit Agreement provides that if S&S as the buyer, requests a refund following the occurrence of a Refund Event, CAC shall refund all pre-delivery payments deposits previously received from S&S within thirty days of receiving notice of the refund request.

9.   S&S made pre-delivery payments and deposits in the amount of $180,000 in accordance with the terms of the Deposit Agreement.

10.   By letter dated October 6, 2012, CAC informed S&S that it was unilaterally increasing the Standard Aircraft Price in an amount of almost $500,000. CAC attached a "Selection Form" to its October 6 letter, requesting S&S to elect one of three options in response to CAC's increase in the Standard Aircraft Price. S&S chose the option to terminate the Deposit Agreement and have all its deposits refunded.

11.   Beginning on October 13, 2012, and continuing thereafter, S&S communicated its decision to terminate the Dealer Agreement and have all its deposits refunded by CAC. CAC acknowledged receipt of S&S's Selection Form and agreed to refund S&S's pre-delivery payments and deposits.

12.   Pursuant to the terms of the Deposit Agreement, CAC was required to refund S&S's pre-delivery payments and deposits within thirty days of receipt of the refund request, on or before December 1, 2012, at the latest. CAC did not refund S&S's pre-delivery payments and deposits on or before December 1, and has not done so to date.

13.   The Deposit Agreement further provides that for litigation commenced in connection with the Deposit Agreement, the prevailing party shall be entitled to reimbursement of its attorneys' fees, expenses and costs.

III.   CLAIMS FOR RELIEF

Claim I.   Breach of Contract

14.   S&S hereby re-alleges and incorporates by reference the allegations in Paragraphs 1 – 13.

15.   CAC has failed to refund to S&S any of its pre-delivery payments and deposits pursuant to the terms of the Deposit Agreement, and thus breached that agreement.

16.   S&S has suffered damages as a result of CAC's breach of the Deposit Agreement.

WHEREFORE, S&S demands judgment against CAC in an amount to be proven at trial, and such other and further relief as may be just, proper and allowable, including its attorneys' fees, pre-judgment and post-judgment interest and the costs of this suit.

Claim II. Unjust Enrichment

17.   S&S hereby re-alleges and incorporates by reference the allegations in Paragraphs 1 – 16.

18.   S&S is entitled to a full refund of all its pre-delivery payments and deposits.

19.   CAC has failed to remit to S&S its pre-delivery payments and deposits, and retained those payments and deposits for itself.

20.   As a result, CAC has been unjustly enriched and has benefited at the direct expense of S&S.

WHEREFORE, S&S demands judgment against CAC in an amount to be proven at trial, and such other and further relief as may be just, proper and allowable, including

4

pre-judgment and post-judgment interest and the costs of this suit.

Claim III. Conversion

21.   S&S hereby re-alleges and incorporates by reference the allegations in Paragraphs 1 – 20.

22.   CAC is in possession of property belonging to S&S, and despite repeated demands, will not return that property.

23.   S&S has suffered damages as a result of CAC's conversion of S&S's property.

WHEREFORE, Sanford & Sons, LTD demands judgment against CAC Corporation in an amount to be proven at trial, and such other and further relief as may be just, proper and allowable, including pre-judgment and post-judgment interest and the costs of this suit.

Dated this 5th Day of December, 2012

Respectfully submitted,

HACKNEY & IMP, LLP

/s/ Mumfort J. Sharken
_____
Lawrence Kimbell
Mumfort J. Sharken Post
Office Box 6842
Hamburg, New York 06000-6842
(555) 555-4734
(555) 555-6043 (facsimile)

ATTORNEYS FOR SANFORD & SONS, LTD.

APPENDIX B:

AN ANSWER

 THE CENTER FOR LEGAL STUDIES

IN THE UNITED STATES DISTRICT COURT

FOR THE

EASTERN DISTRICT OF NEW YORK

SANFORD & SONS LIMITED,
a Swiss Corporation,

Plaintiff,

v.   NO. _____

CAC AVIATION CORPORATION
a New York Corporation,

Defendant.

**DEFENDANT'S ANSWER TO COMPLAINT FOR
BREACH OF CONTRACT, UNJUST
ENRICHMENT, AND CONVERSION**

Defendant CAC Aviation Corporation, a New York corporation ("CAC"), by counsel, for its answer to the plaintiff's Complaint for Breach of Contract, Unjust Enrichment, and Conversion, filed on December 5, 2012 (the "Complaint"), states:

I.   PARTIES AND JURISDICTION

1.   CAC is without knowledge sufficient to admit or deny the allegations in paragraph 1 of the Complaint, and therefore denies the allegations.

2.   CAC admits the allegations in paragraph 2 of the Complaint.

3. CAC admits the allegations in paragraph 3 of the Complaint.

4. CAC is without knowledge sufficient to admit or deny the allegations in paragraph 4 of the Complaint, and therefore denies the allegations.

II. GENERAL ALLEGATIONS

5. In response to the allegations in paragraph 5 of the Complaint, CAC states that agreement referred to speaks for itself, and denies the allegations to the extent inconsistent with the agreement.

6. In response to the allegations in paragraph 6 of the Complaint, CAC states that agreement referred to speaks for itself, and denies the allegations to the extent inconsistent with the agreement.

7. In response to the allegations in paragraph 7 of the Complaint, CAC states that agreement referred to speaks for itself, and denies the allegations to the extent inconsistent with the agreement.

8. In response to the allegations in paragraph 8 of the Complaint, CAC states that agreement referred to speaks for itself, and denies the allegations to the extent inconsistent with the agreement.

9. CAC denies the allegations in paragraph 9 of the Complaint, and states that the timing of the payments was contrary to paragraph 4(A) of the agreement.

10. In response to the allegations in paragraph 10 of the Complaint, CAC states that letter referred to speaks for itself, and denies the allegations to the extent inconsistent with the letter.

11. CAC denies the allegations in paragraph 11 of the Complaint.

12. In response to the allegations in paragraph 12 of the Complaint, CAC states

that agreement referred to speaks for itself, and denies the allegations to the extent inconsistent with the agreement.

13.   In response to the allegations in paragraph 13 of the Complaint, CAC states that agreement referred to speaks for itself, and denies the allegations to the extent inconsistent with the agreement.

CLAIM I.   BREACH OF CONTRACT

14.   In response to paragraph 14 of the Complaint, CAC incorporates by reference its responses to all preceding paragraphs of the Complaint.

15.   In response to the allegations in paragraph 15 of the Complaint, CAC admits that it has not yet paid plaintiff any amounts due or to become due, but denies the remaining allegations in paragraph 15 of the Complaint.

16.   CAC denies the allegations in paragraph 16 of the Complaint.

CLAIM II. UNJUST ENRICHMENT

17.   In response to paragraph 17 of the Complaint, CAC incorporates by reference its responses to all preceding paragraphs of the Complaint.

18.   CAC denies the allegations in paragraph 18 of the Complaint.

19.   CAC denies the allegations in paragraph 19 of the Complaint.

20.   CAC denies the allegations in paragraph 20 of the Complaint.

CLAIM III. CONVERSION

21.   In response to paragraph 21 of the Complaint, CAC incorporates by reference its responses to all preceding paragraphs of the Complaint.

22.   CAC denies the allegations in paragraph 22 of the Complaint.

23.   CAC denies the allegations in paragraph 23 of the Complaint.

24.   CAC denies all allegations not specifically admitted in this answer.

FIRST AFFIRMATIVE DEFENSE

CAC asserts the defense of partial setoff, because the funds sent by Plaintiff were not sent or received by the deadlines set forth in paragraph 4(A) of the subject agreement.

SECOND AFFIRMATIVE DEFENSE

Plaintiff's conversion claim fails to state a claim upon which relief can be granted.

WHEREFORE, CAC requests that Plaintiff take nothing by its Complaint, for costs, and for all other just and proper relief.

Dated: December 27, 2012

Respectfully submitted,

David L. Carlson
David L. Carlson
Attorney for the Defendant
500 Main St. N.W., Suite 120
Orchard Park, NY 06001
(555) 555-9164
(555) 555-8472 (fax)

CERTIFICATE OF SERVICE

I, David L. Carlson, hereby certify that I am the attorney for the Defendant, CAC Aviation Corporation and served copies of Defendant's Answer to Complaint on the following parties by way of courier on December 27, 2012:

Lawrence Kimbell, Esq.   698 Lawrence Blvd. Hamburg, New York 06000

Mumfort J. Sharken, Esq. 698 Lawrence Blvd. Hamburg, New York 06000

I certify that the foregoing is true and correct.

DATED: 12/27/2012

David T. Carlson
_____
Signature

APPENDIX C:

INTERROGATORIES

THE CENTER FOR
LEGAL STUDIES

STATE OF NEW YORK
SUPREME COURT: COUNTY OF ERIE

SAM DeMANN,

        Plaintiff,

                                                        REQUEST FOR
                                         INTERROGATORIES

        v.
                                          Index No: _____

POLLY KETTLE'S TEA EMPORIUM,

        Defendant,

Plaintiff requests that Defendant respond to the following interrogatories separately and fully in writing and under oath, pursuant to § 2030 of the New York Code of Civil Procedure, and that the response be signed by the person making them and be returned to Richard Smith at the Law Offices of Smith, Browne and Jones, 100 First Avenue, Buffalo, New York, 00000 within thirty (30) days after service of these interrogatories.

DEFINITIONS AND INSTRUCTIONS

(Omitted For Example Purposes)

INTERROGATORIES

1. Please identify the person or persons responding to these Interrogatories on behalf of the defendant, and identify each person who has provided information in connection with these Interrogatories.

2. Identify any person not already named as party to the suit whom you contend caused or contributed to the occurrence complained of, including any architect, engineer, designer, contractor, subcontractor or others.

3. Identify each person with whom you are aware that:

    a. Witnessed the incident or the events occurring immediately before and after the incident; and /or who

    b. Heard any statements made about the incident by any individual at the scene.

4. Identify each employee with personal knowledge of the incident.

    a. For each individual, identify his or her job title and job or function which was being performed by the individual at time of the incident.

5. Identify each person interviewed concerning the incident. For each person, state:

    a. The date of the interview.

    b. The substance of the interview.

    c. If the interview was recorded and/or transcribed, a reproduction of the recording and/or transcript will suffice.

6. Identify each and every written report made by any person concerning the incident.

7. Please state, in your own words, what you believe happened to plaintiff on the common walkway in front of the premises located at 9 Tremont Way, Buffalo, New York, on January 12, 2013 and include in your answer the bases upon which you have formed that belief.

8. Identify any insurance agreement(s) under which any insurance business may be liable to satisfy part or all of any judgment which may be entered in this action, or to indemnify or reimburse you for payments made to satisfy the judgment, including in your answer the amount in limits of any such liability insurance coverage.

14   9. Identify any previous or subsequent incidents of which or where which occurred in

substantially the same manner as the incident complained of in this lawsuit at the premises of

9 Tremont Way, Buffalo, New York.

15   10. At the time of plaintiff's injury, do you contend that any person or entity other than you

manage the premises and which plaintiff alleges he was injured and, if so, state each and

every fact upon which you base the contention and identify each and every writing that

supports that contention.

Dated: Buffalo, NY
      May 29, 2013

Respectfully submitted,

By:_____
      Richard Smith
Attorney for Plaintiff
100 First Avenue
Buffalo, NY 00000

CERTIFICATE OF SERVICE

I, Richard Smith, attorney for Plaintiff do hereby certify that a true and correct copy of the Plaintiff's Request for Interrogatories was served, upon Counsel to Defendant via electronic mail and by first class mail via U.S. Postal Service to the last known address known to me this ____day of_____, 2____ addressed as follows:

Regina Randolph, Registration #667
6868 Pothole Rd.
Amherst, NY 00101
(555)555-5551

APPENDIX D:

REQUEST FOR ADMISSIONS

THE CENTER FOR
LEGAL STUDIES

STATE OF NEW YORK
SUPREME COURT: COUNTY OF ERIE

SAM DeMANN,

        Plaintiff,

                                         REQUEST FOR
                                         ADMISSIONS

        vs.   Index No: _____

POLLY KETTLE'S TEA EMPORIUM,

        Defendant,

        Plaintiff requests that Defendant respond to the following request for admissions separately and in writing and verified under oath, pursuant to § 2033 of the CPLR, at the Law Offices of Smith, Browne and Jones, 100 First Avenue, Buffalo, New York, 00000 within thirty (30) days after service of these requests.

        FAILURE TO TIMELY SERVE WITH VERIFIED RESPONSES, DEFENDANT SHALL WAIVE OBJECTIONS AND PRIVILEGES AND THE REQUESTS MAY BE DEEMED ADMITTED.

    1.   Admit that on January 12, 2013, defendant, Polly Kettle's Tea Emporium, was a corporation organized and existing under the laws of the State of New York, and had its principal place of business at 9 Tremont Way, in the City of Buffalo, County of Erie, State of New York.

    2.   Admit that on January 12, 2013, defendant, Polly Kettle's Tea Emporium, was the owner and lessor of a building located at 9 Tremont Way, in the City of Buffalo, County of Erie, State of New York.

3.   Admit that on January 12, 2013, defendant had in effect a policy of insurance, through which you were or might be insured in any manner of liability, with Acme Insurance Company, 356 Insurance Drive, Buffalo, New York 00000.

4.   Admit that on January 12, 2013, defendant was open for business to receive employees, customers or other persons.

5.   Admit that defendant was aware of city ordinance, § (i) 8.03.01 that requires businesses to keep the sidewalks in front of their stores reasonably clear from all hazards.

6.   Admit that on January 12, 2013, defendant was aware of the hazardous condition of the sidewalk and entrance to defendant's place of business.

7.   Admit that the Plaintiff did require necessary medical treatment as a result of the incident that took place on January 12, 2013.

8.   Admit that defendant placed salt on the sidewalk and entrance to defendant's business in lieu of snow removal.

9.   Admit that Polly Kettle's Tea Emporium has not basis to assert as s defense or affirmative defense that the Plaintiff assumed the risk of his injuries.

10.   Admit that Polly Kettle's Tea Emporium maintained insurance that covers its liability in this lawsuit.

Respectfully submitted,

Dated: Buffalo, NY
June 10, 2013

By:_____
Richard Smith
Attorney for Plaintiff
100 First Avenue
Buffalo, NY 00000

CERTIFICATE OF SERVICE

I, Richard Smith, attorney for Plaintiff do hereby certify that a true and correct copy of the Plaintiff's Request for Admissions was served, upon Counsel to Defendant via electronic mail and by first class mail via U.S. Postal Service to the last known address known to me this _____ day of _____, 2___ addressed as follows:

Regina Randolph, Registration #667
6868 Pothole Rd.
Amherst, NY 00101
(555)555-5551

APPENDIX E:

REQUEST FOR PRODUCTION OF DOCUMENTS

THE CENTER FOR
LEGAL STUDIES

STATE OF NEW YORK
SUPREME COURT: COUNTY OF ERIE

SAM DeMANN,

       Plaintiff,

REQUEST FOR PRODUCTION OF DOCUMENTS

       vs.

Index No: _____

POLLY KETTLE'S TEA EMPORIUM,

       Defendant,

     Pursuant to § 2031 of the New York Code of Civil Procedure, Plaintiffs, by and through their attorneys, hereby demand that the Defendant produce for discovery, inspecting and copying at the Law Offices of Smith, Browne and Jones, 100 First Avenue, Buffalo, New York, 00000, the following documents and material.

INSTRUCTIONS

(Omitted For Example Purposes)

DOCUMENTS TO BE PRODUCED

1.   Provide legible copies of each insurance policy for Polly Kettle's Tea Emporium.

2.   Provide all photographs, videotapes or audio tapes, x-rays, diagrams, surveys or other graphic representations of information concerning the subject matter of this action, the Plaintiff, or property damage.

3.   Provide copies of all documents supporting each denial of a material allegation in your pleadings.

4. Provide copies of all documents supporting your contention that plaintiff contributed to his own injuries.

5. Provide copies of any written or recorded statement given by persons in supporting your contention that you were in compliance with city ordinance (i) 8.03.01.

6. Provide copies of any and every document, citation or publication, relative to city ordinance (i) 8.03.01.

7. Provide any documents identified in any other parties' Answers to Interrogatories.

8. Provide any documents received pursuant to a subpoena request.

9. Provide any document prepared during the regular course of business as a result of the incident complained of in the Plaintiff's Complaint.

10. Provide any treaties, standards in the industry, legal authority, rule, case, statute or code that will be relied upon in the defense of this case.

Dated: Buffalo, NY
        June 6, 2013

Respectfully submitted,

By:_____
    Richard Smith
    Attorney for Plaintiff
    100 First Avenue
    Buffalo, NY 00000

CERTIFICATE OF SERVICE

I, Richard Smith, attorney for Plaintiff do hereby certify that a true and correct copy of the Plaintiff's Request for Documents Production was served, upon Counsel to Defendant via electronic mail and by first class mail via U.S. Postal Service to the last known address known to me this _____ day of _____, 2____ addressed as follows:

Regina Randolph, Registration #667
6868 Pothole Rd.
Amherst, NY 00101
(555)555-5551

INDEX

THE CENTER FOR
LEGAL STUDIES

INDEX